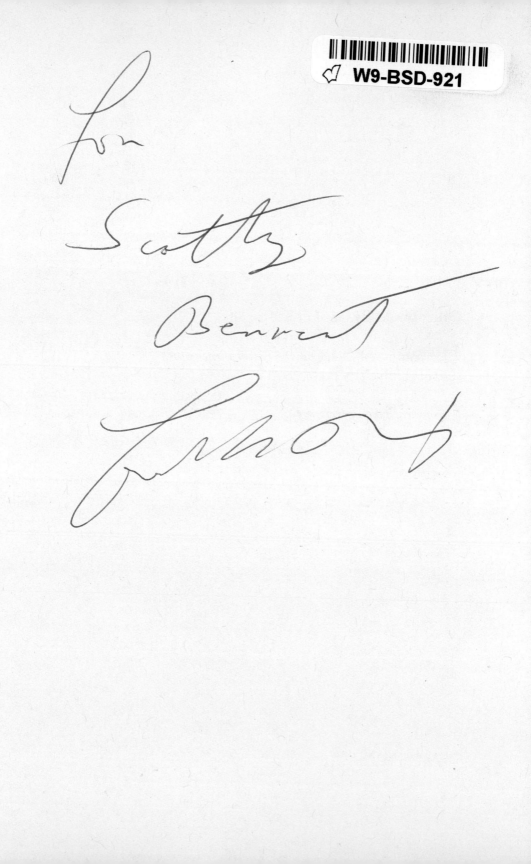

For
Scotty
Bennett

Other Books By Gordon K. Durnil:

The Making of a Conservative Environmentalist
Indiana University Press, 1995

Is America Beyond Reform?
Sligo Press, 1997

THROWING CHAIRS AND RAISING HELL
Politics in the Bulen Era

Gordon K. Durnil

In Conjunction with
The Bulen Symposium On American Politics
Indiana University Purdue University Indianapolis

Guild Press of Indiana
Carmel, IN 46032

Dedication

This book is dedicated to one of those men who occasionally come along in American life and change the course of history.

Some of these men serve as governmental leaders and statesmen, and a few others, normally unrecognized, serve as polictical organizational leaders.

L. Keith Bulen, of Indianapolis, Indiana served as both.

Table of Contents

WHAT OTHERS SAY:

We Miss Leaders Like Keith Bulen

Our party has been blessed with some very able, dedicated people. I can think of no one who has done more over the years for the Republican Party than Keith Bulen.

Keith was a joy for me to work with. He was strong and tough. His great sense of humor often carried the day during difficult negotiations.

Keith gave so much to the Republican Party. In these days when politics have become so contentious—sometimes downright ugly—we all miss leaders like Keith Bulen.

George Bush

This tribute is from the viewpoint of an extraordinary career of jobs ranging from Republican County Chairman to the 41st President of the United States.

Lawrence Keith Bulen
A Brief Summary of a Distinguished Career

Born in Madison County, Indiana, on New Year's Eve of 1926, L. Keith Bulen began his primary education in the depths of the Great Depression and graduated from Pendleton High School in 1944 at the height of World War II. He joined the U.S. Army Air Corps and launched a lengthy service to his nation.

Keith studied government and earned his Bachelors Degree in 1949 and Doctor of Jurisprudence in 1952, both from Indiana University, and he practiced law as the senior member of Bulen, Castor, Robinette & Nickels in Indianapolis. His progeny are daughters Leslie K., Lisa K., L. Kassee, and L. Kellee, along with granddaughters, Lawren K. Mills and Lindsey K. Rodda.

For nearly a half century, Keith Bulen served as a political and governmental leader. He was elected or appointed to serve at the block, precinct, ward, county, district, state, national, and international levels. As Marion County Republican Chairman, he brought not just victory, but openness, respect, fun, and accountability to the Republican Party.

Keith Bulen cultivated the initial successes of a great statesman, Richard G. Lugar, and furthered the careers of such other great public servants as Bill Ruckelshaus, Bill Hudnut, John Mutz, and Bob Orr, while attracting a remarkably talented and diverse group of individuals to other positions in public service. He helped give birth to metropolitan government (Uni-Gov), brought attention and honor to Indianapolis, and took the management of campaigns for Congress, governor and President to unprecedented levels of organization.

In the 1960s and 1970s, Keith provided the impetus for the revitalization of the Indiana Republican Party, but his true political legacy lies in the generations of leaders who were taught by a premier mentor to express their love of country and principle through a devotion to a vigorous two-party system and a free electoral process.

His successes were not limited to law and politics. President Ronald Reagan appointed Keith, and the U.S. Senate confirmed him, as a Commissioner of the International Joint Commission, a treaty organization tasked with resolving and preventing problems between the United States and Canada. In this role, Keith was praised for resolving a major boundary water dispute between the State of Washington and the Province of British Columbia.

Keith also achieved success as a horse owner and breeder. He led the Indiana Standardbred Association and was inducted into their Hall of Fame. His world champion pacer, Abercrombie, was voted Harness Horse of the Year in 1978.

A man of honor, achievement, and versatility, L. Keith Bulen will always be remembered as one of Indiana's finest and most dedicated native sons. He succumbed to cancer in the early morning hours of January 4, 1999.

Downright Ugly

President George Bush speaks of contemporary politics as "so contentious—sometimes downright ugly." Then he says, "We all miss leaders like Keith Bulen."

So, what kind of leader was he?

Therein lies the underlying question for this book and a reason for instituting the annual Bulen Symposium On American Politics. The time is ripe to initiate debate on the way politics used to be and the way it now is. Was it better in the Bulen era, or better now? If it has worsened, why did that happen? Maybe politics are merely mirrors of the evolutionary cycles of American culture. Clearly, both our culture and the practice of politics have undergone dramatic change in the final decades of the twentieth century.

Television certainly changed the expectations and judgments of Americans in numerous ways. We have learned to expect answers for almost any problem within a thirty or sixty minute time frame. We tend to judge entertainment celebrities, candidates, and office holders, equally–more on appearance than substance. Cable television and the 24 hour news cycle could be a reason for the rapid change in political attitudes of the 1990s as the partisan blaring chases more and more of us away from giving the body politic a place of significance in our lives. A decline in the respect given to civility in our society could certainly be a culprit. More than anything else, in the judgment of your author, the decline in importance of the traditional American two party system is what has brought on the "ugliness" mentioned by George Bush. As the influence of party organization waned, so did the responsibility and accountability of elected officials.

Keith Bulen was an organizational politician operating in Indiana, which was then an organizational state. Hoosiers took politics seriously. From the time when Abraham Lincoln explained how a winning campaign must be organized, serious politicians set out to perfect his plan.

Lincoln's plan was simple, as are most serious campaign plans. He said that an organized candidacy would canvas every household in the appropriate district, county, or state. Each person would be asked whether or not he or she supported the candidate, and, if they did, the campaign should make sure all of those favorable voters actually voted on election day. For one hundred years, politicians improved upon the Lincoln plan, by electing precinct committeemen to canvas the households; by making sure favorable voters were registered to vote; by using mail, telephones, computers, and every other appropriate new invention over the years to "rifle shot" individual voters in the identification and election day turnout process.

Then we let it go.

In the Bulen era, especially in the Lugar mayoral campaigns, organizational politics reached their zenith. Bulen crossed every T and dotted every I. Nothing was left to chance. Surprises were not tolerated. Missing deadlines was not accepted, even from volunteers. Every doorbell was rung, every household canvassed, every favorable voter wooed. Are there any kids at college who need absentee ballots? Are any elderly family members in nursing homes? Anyone in the hospital? What time should the volunteer arrive to give the voter a ride to the polls? No group of voters were ignored, none taken for granted.

More examples of organizational politics follow in The Bulen Era which was written in 1972 as a Christmas gift to Keith Bulen. Within those pages you will find the "cat story" as an illustration of the way Bulen organized volunteer activity.

Organized political activity in the Bulen era relied on volunteers, and maybe that is another reason for political party decline. In a society where Mom and Dad both work all day and worry about the well being of their children at night, little time is left for politics. And just maybe Mom and Dad don't care much about politics. Maybe they think politicians are similar to entertainers who can be viewed from afar and who are merely ego driven men and women who have little bearing on the lives of busy mom and dads. They somehow forget that the schools their kids attend and the lessons they learn, the roads on which they drive to work, the taxes they pay, the sewers into which they flush their waste, all connect them to politics every day of their lives.

In the Bulen era the opponent was respected. Political antagonists could battle hard for an advantage, but in a civil manner. Bill Hudnut and Andy Jacobs were both congressmen from the same district and they opposed each other in two hotly contested elections. Both conducted themselves as gentlemen as Hudnut won in 1972 and Jacobs won in 1974. And in the words of Democrat Andy Jacobs, Republican Bulen helped to make politics fun.

In the Bulen era, democratic debate was an essential element of our freedoms, as it had been for centuries. One side promoted one view, the other side an opposing view. Typically, compromise made both sides a little happy and a little sad, but the people were well served. As we move to the next millennium, compromise connotes defeat,—even "selling out" your principles. Democratic debate has become a hysterical "yelling and screaming" contest on cable television stations among people with big mouths and little ears.

Noticeable among the commentary by those who have written their remembrances of Keith Bulen, is a worry that we might not have such leaders in the future. These people, who have individually proven that one person can make a difference in this nation of which they are so proud, fear that people of dedication and talent might not step forward to insure that we have decent people in government, and that we will not have citizens willing to do the volunteer work necessary to elect good people. They worry that we might not see again the type of political leaders we have seen in the past.

Are their fears well founded? Contemporary evidence seems to be on that side of the argument. But then most politicians lean toward pessimism. Keith Bulen always believed that if we don't do all of the things that need to be done, we will lose. The optimist might say, "if we do all that we must do, we will win." For politicians, losing –rather than winning–seems to be the better motivator to get the necessary work done. So perhaps the fear that qualified leaders will not step forward, will cause some to do just that.

Your author first met Keith Bulen in the early sixties. In 1964, I was a candidate for state representative on the Goldwater ticket and he was a state representative not seeking re-election. We began working together in 1965 and continued to do so for the next thirty five years or so. In 1972 I wrote *The Bulen Era* as a Christmas gift to Keith. It was my view of his time at the helm. Because of our close working relationship, I knew a lot, but not all, about his successful stewardship. Hopefully, as you read *The Bulen Era,* you will get a good idea about Keith's outstanding organizational abilities, and the need for good people to volunteer. Following *The Bulen Era* are a series of essays written by his colleagues. Occasionally, the author cannot resist from making a comment. Finally, is the offer of basic campaign advice should you or a colleague decide to seek public office.

Keith Bulen was unique, but there have been other great political leaders. Who will be next to take the lead? How about you? Every generation needs only a few. Perhaps the annual Bulen Symposium On American Politics will light the fire in the bellies of a few individuals who will take on the responsibility of political leadership in the future. Such is the hope of the organizers of The Bulen Symposium on American Politics.

Let's take a look back to yesteryear when "politics were politics."

"The Bulen Era"

Prior to 1967, the Republican Party in Marion County, Indiana had generated many victorious campaigns. The Republican voters were concentrated primarily in the suburban areas of the county, while the Democratic strength was mostly found within the Indianapolis city limits. The odds for winning a county wide election were favorable, but winning a city election had become a near impossibility for the Republican Party. After World War I, a Republican mayor became a novel experience—John L. Duvall, was elected in 1925, another Republican, Robert Tyndall, was elected in 1943, and, in 1951, Republican Alex M. Clark was elected. From 1925 through 1967, Indianapolis had twelve Democrat mayors and only four Republicans.

In 1967, however, Indianapolis voters were exposed to an invigorated Republican Party. A fresh candidate, Richard G. Lugar, came onto the scene with the support of the newly reorganized Marion County Republican Central Committee. Lugar was a candidate unlike any of his predecessors. He was highly educated, honest, dedicated, as well as successful in business and in community service. He was a candidate who had the foresight and the courage to say, and mean, that the people of Indianapolis could meet and solve the awesome urban problems of the late sixties and early seventies. He was young, articulate, well informed, and he made an attractive candidate. The people of the city could relate to this man who knew and understood their problems and who offered constructive solutions.

Richard G. Lugar was elected mayor of Indianapolis in 1967, and his promises soon became reality. But we need to take a look at the political organization that Lugar relied upon to assist him toward his party's nomination and his subsequent election. His primary election opponent was former Republican mayor, Alex M. Clark, a tough competitor and an old pro in county politics. In the general election that fall, Lugar faced another old pro, the incumbent Democrat Mayor, John J. Barton. Lugar and the young Marion County Republican Organization were the underdogs in both battles, but underdogs with a strong desire for good government, and an unusual willingness to give of their time, ability, and money to pursue their cause. The concentrated teamwork and cooperation of Marion County Republicans under the leadership of L. Keith Bulen won both battles.

By the mid-sixties, the Marion County Republican Organization had been under the able leadership of County Chairman H. Dale Brown for many years. Brown had served as Republican chairman of the 11th Congressional District and briefly as Indiana Republican State Chairman. He was the dean of Republican leadership in Indiana, but he had sustained several recent losses and Marion County Republicans were not fond of losing. In the early sixties several non-organization candidates were able to beat the primary slate published by the Republican Organization under Brown's leadership. One such candidate was State Representative L. Keith Bulen.

In 1964 a group of conservative candidates under the label of the Republican Victory Committee, and closely tied to the Presidential candidacy of Barry Goldwater, were able to defeat the majority of Brown's primary election ticket. 1964 was not a good year for Republicans nationally, and the Republican Party in Marion County lost every race with the exception of Juvenile Court Judge. 1958 had been another bad year, but the county G.O.P. was especially disorganized following the 1964 loss.

Republican Action Committee

In 1965, Marion County Republicans began a series of meetings attempting to resolve the party's problems. Their goal was to put Republicans back on the winning track. The group consisted of office holders, former office holders, party supporters, as well as ward and precinct leaders. The name chosen for the new committee was the Republican Action Committee. They formed an executive committee made up of Charles Applegate, Dr. Lawrence Borst, James A. Buck, L. Keith Bulen, John Burkhart, Thomas Hasbrook, Mrs. Marcia Hawthorne, W. W. Hill, Jr., Edwin Koch, Judge John Niblack, Noble Pearcy, Lewis Ping, William T. Ray, William D. Ruckelshaus,[1] Beurt SerVaas, John Sutton and Miss Phyllis Waters. The committee began soliciting members at $2.00 per person, not just to raise funds, which were needed, but to give the members a stake in the success of the committee. Membership card number one was issued to John Burkhart on April 23, 1965. By May 14th card number 300 had been issued to Silas B. Reagan, and by Christmas, 1965, Ada F. Harvey was the one thousandth paid member, as the effort grew in size and determination.

L. Keith Bulen was elected chairman and, from that point in 1965, the Republican Action Committee went into a precisely executed strategy to change control of the Republican Party in Marion County, with the goal of electing Bulen as chairman at the county convention to be held on the Saturday following the primary election in May of 1966.

Indiana was an extremely well organized state politically, and the success of almost any candidate ultimately rested in the hands of the precinct committeeman at the neighborhood level. Even prior to 1967, in terms of Republican activity, Marion County was one of the best organized counties in the state. These same precinct committeemen and vice committeemen were the electorate who would elect the county chairman. The Action Committee, and Bulen in particular, began an intensive campaign to contact each precinct committeeman and vice committeeman. He pledged a professional political organization based upon honesty and integrity. Bulen also promised professional audits of all committee receipts and expenditures, and to make such audits available for public scrutiny.

Bulen promised to seek out the best qualified candidates available to run on the Republican ticket. He fielded candidates who represented all social, geographical, racial, religious, and philosophical segments of the greater Indianapolis community. The old method of selecting the party's suggested nominees had been a slating convention, which had attracted to it all the bad connotations of old time bossism politics. In preparing for the 1966 primary election, Bulen called upon a group of community leaders, representing all segments of the Republican Party, to form a screening committee which would recommend highly qualified candidates for public office. Any person desiring to be a candidate had the opportunity to appear before the screening committee and state his or her case. The screening committee concept was extremely successful in 1966, as it was in every Marion County election under Bulen's leadership.

Selected by that first screening committee were such candidates as Prosecutor Noble Pearcy and the following judicial candidates: Charles C. Daugherty, Wilbur H. Grant, Glenn F. Funk, Frank A. Symmes, Jr., Addison M. Dowling, Rufus C. Kuykendall Charles W. Applegate, Edward Madinger, John T. Davis and Saul I. Rabb. Also selected were State Senators Leslie Duvall and W. W. Hill, Jr., and State Representatives Walter H. Barbour, Lawrence M. Borst, Charles E. Bosma, Danny L. Burton,[2] Harriett B. Conn, Ray P. Crowe, William J. Fay, Richard G. Givan,[3] Robert L. Jones, Jr., Eugene H. Lamkin, Jr., John M. Mutz,[4] Paul S. Partlow, Richard Retterer, William D. Ruckelshaus and Otis M. Yarnell.

Recommended for county offices were E. Allen Hunter, Clerk; John T. Sutton, Auditor; Marcia M. Hawthorne, Recorder; William S. Mercuri, Assessor; Lewis R. Ping, Commissioner; and Beurt R. SerVaas, Councilman. Also selected with that team was 11th District Congressional Candidate Paul Oakes, with a young man named Dick Lugar as his campaign manager.

Bulen recognized that the Republican Party was not making

sufficient inroads with youth. The Marion County Young Republican Organization had not functioned effectively for several years, so Bulen established a counter-organization under the name of Young Republicans For Action. The Y. R. A. was allowed to elect their own officers, a fundamental right that was not permitted in the official Young Republican Organization. Danny L. Burton was elected as Y. R. A. Chairman. Other charter officers were Marilyn Horsley, Dr. Eugene H. Lamkin, Jr., Donna Schubert, Sharon Delph, Alice Armantrout, Carol Claffey, Gordon K. Durnil and Lynda Smith. The Y.R.A. grew by the hundreds and was another important factor in the Action Committee movement.

During the turbulent early months of 1966, Marion County had two well organized Republican County committees. The official committee maintained a full-time office on the third floor of a downtown building, somewhat hidden from the public. Bulen brought the Action Committee headquarters to the people, by opening a full-time office on the ground floor of a busy downtown street. It was a political headquarters that was easily accessible to volunteers.

As May, 1966 approached, the stage was set for two important battles. The first was the primary election to be held on the first Tuesday following the first Monday in May. The first battle pitted the Action Committee team of candidates against the official Republican slate. Through the efforts of thousands of dedicated volunteers, assembled by Bulen and others working with him, each and every Action Committee county-wide candidate was victorious. Another key front of the primary battle was the election of Republican precinct committeemen, for it was the committeemen who would determine who would be the Republican county chairman for the next two years. Again, on that front, the Action Committee was victorious in electing a strong team of precinct officials.

The second battle occurred on the Saturday next following the primary election. It was a confrontation between the old pro, H. Dale Brown, a master politician, against L. Keith Bulen, a young attractive, articulate, highly successful attorney, who had never lost an election. Both were experienced in the political facts of life, and both knew how to count votes in advance of the convention. Convention day was anti-climatic. Brown knew he was beaten and withdrew from the race. Bulen became the Chairman of the Marion County Republican Central Committee. It is from that point in time that Indianapolis became known nationally as a center of leadership for the Republican Party.

---

1. Bill Ruckelshaus twice served as Administrator of the Environmental Protection Agency under Presidents Nixon and Reagan.
2. Dan Burton later served as a Member of Congress from the Sixth District of Indiana.
3. Dick Given later served as the Chief Justice of the Indiana Supreme Court.
4. John Mutz later served as Lieutenant Governor of the state of Indiana.
5. Gordon Durnil later served eight years as the Chairman of the Indiana Republican Party.

Chapter Two

The summer of 1966 was a time for a significant metamorphosis in Hoosier Republican politics.

Politically, Marion County was subdivided into a number of townships and wards, which were geographical areas made up of a number of precincts. Each had a chairman and vice-chairman who oversaw the performance of precinct committeemen and vice-committeemen. Pre-Bulen, ward chairmen had always been appointed by the County Chairman of their respective political parties. Under such a system, assuming that the ward chairman could influence his precinct committeemen, it was not difficult for a county chairman to perpetuate himself in office.

As county chairman, Keith Bulen wanted most of all to strengthen the Republican Party. To do so, he believed that the party must be responsive not only to the leadership within the party, but to the people in their neighborhoods. Under Indiana law, the primary election voters elected the precinct committeemen, and the committeemen (with their appointed vice committeemen) elected the county chairman, but there was no direct link between the people and their ward chairman. Bulen established the policy of allowing the precinct committeemen to elect their own ward chairmen. The result of that policy was a stronger and more responsive Republican Party in Indianapolis.

Another Bulen innovation was publishing a monthly, six-page, newsletter. The purpose of the publication was to keep Republicans informed with factual information about the purpose and direction of the party. It also served as a sounding board for new ideas, as a method for recognizing the accomplishments of party workers, and to provide notice of Republican meetings within the county. In naming Gordon K. Durnil, an Indianapolis attorney, as editor of the Marion County *Republican Reporter*, Bulen gave the instructions that this publication was to be the best of its kind in the country.

The first issue of *The Republican Reporter* was published in June, 1966. The front page of that first issue carried a smiling former Vice President of the United States who had been in Indianapolis campaigning on behalf of Hoosier Republican Congressmen. That former Vice President had been a long time friend of Hoosiers, and had visited the State many times. His mother was born in Jennings County, Indiana, and, of course, he was the Honorable Richard M. Nixon. Within several months after beginning publication, Ray Bliss, the Republican National Chairman, commended Marion County on its outstanding newsletter, and requested extra copies to be sent to other Republican county chairmen around the nation as an example for them to emulate. *The Republican Reporter* was circulated extensively in Marion County, and to Republican leaders throughout the state of Indiana, the nation, and the world.

As County Chairman, Bulen immediately pursued those groups who were considered solid block votes for the Democrats. Inroads were made with minority groups, with labor, and with youth. He brought computerization and data processing into use as a political tool, and the Marion County Republican Headquarters sported its own data processing equipment shortly after such equipment came on the market.

The Republican State Committee was made up of the chairmen and vice-chairmen of the eleven Congressional Districts within the state. The county chairmen in each district elected the district chairmen and vice-chairmen. Since all of the 11th Congressional District was within Marion County, it was up to Bulen to select the district officers for that district. He chose Miss Nola A. Allen, as the 11th District Vice-Chairman. An attorney, Miss Allen became the first member of the Negro race to serve on the Indiana Republican State Central Committee. She later became the first woman to serve as a district chairman on the same committee.

The 1966 general election was a critical one for Bulen and the Republican Party. Following the 1964 disaster, it was a fact that if the Democrats should win the election, there would be no Republican county officials left in office. The local news media predicted that the election was a toss-up, and that the party with the best organization would win. The Republican Party, under the leadership of Keith Bulen, won big. It was clear that Bulen had the best political organization in the state—perhaps the best in the nation. The reason for the excellent organization was also clear. The ability and dedication of the precinct committeemen and grassroots workers who were doing their thing for the cause of good government, and not for personal reward, was certainly a key factor. In those days, elections were won or lost at the neighborhood level where volunteers could campaign directly with voters, not just on television or in the news media, and it took an outstanding leader to inspire the workers to do their thing. Marion County Republicans had such a leader.

In the December, 1966, issue of *The Republican Reporter* appeared the following quote:

> *Political leaders have a tendency to surround themselves with aides who are not capable of challenging them for leadership of the party, the result being an average organization. Under the dynamic and intelligent leadership of L. Keith Bulen, such is not the case. Keith has put into positions of importance Republicans of the highest intelligence, fortitude, and desire to work hard for victory. Many of whom would made good contenders for his job. By surrounding himself with such people, he is achieving his desired result— success for the Republican Party in Marion County, in Indiana, and nationally.*

The new Republican leadership had the courage to bring about change in the party, the ability to mold into a team all segments of the party, and an unusual savvy for organizational politics. They also had a burning desire to win and were extremely successful in their first campaign year of 1966, winning almost every office on the ballot. Chairman Bulen was now looking ahead to 1967, and the challenge of electing the first Republican mayor in Indianapolis since 1951.

Chapter Three

Almost every campaign manual refers to the three-legged stool as an example of the tools necessary for a successful campaign. The first leg of the stool is a good political organization, the second leg is an outstanding candidate, and sufficient finances is the third leg. As the New Year of 1967 dawned on Indianapolis, an effective political organization was in existence and Bulen was considering an extremely talented young man as a potential candidate, but the financial prospects were not so good. Few potential contributors expected a Republican victory in a city election and many contributors preferred to contribute to probable winners. Few were then or are now willing to support apparent losers.

The odds were strongly against a Republican being elected as mayor of Indianapolis, irrespective of who the candidate might be. The 1966 county wide victory had perked up the Republican Party, as it should since there were more Democrats in the county than there were Republicans. A professional survey of voter opinion revealed that 34.3 percent of Marion County voters were behavior Republicans, while 43.0 per cent were Democrats, and 17.9 per cent were ticket splitters with the remainder marginal. Center Township was the largest populated of the nine townships in Marion County, and in 1967 it contained the largest number of voters in the city. From the survey referred to above, 24.1 per cent of the voters in Center Township were behavior Republicans, while 44.7 per cent were behavior Democrats. All of that was clear evidence that a Republican victory in the city of Indianapolis in 1967 was improbable.

Even in the face of such odds, three prominent Republicans declared their intent to seek the Republican nomination for mayor. Each of the three had significant following within the Marion County Republican Organization and the question was raised—can the newly reorganized political organization recommend any one of the three, and still hold the organization together? Will the team, consisting of all the various wings of the party, hold together, or will it split asunder because the candidate representing one faction or the other was not recommended?

One of these candidates, Judge William T. Sharp, had previously been a candidate for mayor and was a leader of the Republican Victory Committee in 1964. Another, as previously mentioned, was former mayor Alex M. Clark, the last Republican to be elected. The third candidate didn't have the pre-existing political following of the other two. Richard G. Lugar had served as vice president of the Indianapolis Board of School Commissioners and had been the leading member of the committee supporting a Republican Congressional candidate in 1966.

County Chairman Bulen again relied on the screening committee concept to select the best possible candidates for city offices. In the February, 1967, issue of *The Republican Reporter* appeared the following appeal to party workers.

> *Being the party of the people, we are asking for your recommendations for city candidates in 1967. This November we have the opportunity to elect a Republican Mayor, City Clerk, and a two-thirds majority of the city council, IF we nominate the best possible ticket in the primary this May.*
>
> *The candidates recommendation committee will interview every person of whose interest they are made aware, and will do its very best to build a winning team for November. Mr. John Burkhart, committee chairman, is asking all good Republicans to suggest names of those persons who are interested in running for city office.*

Serving as members of the candidates recommendation committee were Rex Early,[1] Marcia Hawthorne, J. B. King, Robert Morris, Marjorie Nackenhorst, John Niblack, Noble Pearcy, Richard Petticrew, and Harold Ransburg. Also serving were John Sutton, Don Tabbert, Phyllis Waters, Doris L. Dorbecker, Helen Rotzien and John Sweezy.[2] The screening committee met, considered all candidates, and deliberated long hours before agreeing that one man was far superior and far more qualified than any candidate that had appeared before them. They selected Dick Lugar as the recommended candidate for the Republican nomination in the mayor's race. Judge Sharp withdrew and threw his support to former Mayor Clark. And the battle lines were set. The young and exciting Dick Lugar who spoke of the future, and Alex Clark, a man who had been mayor of Indianapolis and who displayed a proven record, went to the post.

The selection of Dick Lugar was a surprise to the many GOP team members who did not know him. Many who did know of him were concerned because as a school board member Lugar had been a leader in solving many problems, racial and otherwise, within the school system. To some this made him controversial. Those Republicans who had met him and talked with him, however, had little doubt that here was a man who could change the destiny of Indianapolis, and perhaps of the nation.

In March, 1967 issue of *The Republican Reporter* appeared these quotes:

> *In the annals of Marion County politics there can be found many men who may be described by the adjective astute. Records will also show candidates and organizational leaders whose insight seemed almost phenomenal in dealing with political repertoire. It is quite wonderful, however, that each and every campaign brings to light an untouched resource of energy, knowledge, personality, spunk, know-how, and in general, outstanding candidate qualities that are so very much needed by our constantly changing party make-up today.*

> *Questions are bombarding all sides of our elected officials, the central committee, and Republicans in the City-County Building. Mostly they say that Lugar is not well known, and to this the questioner should hang a shameful head. This would show that they are spending too much time in the sports section or on the funnies, and too little with the portion of the newspaper devoted to who is getting things done in Indianapolis today. Proof of performance shows that Lugar is the leader we need now.*

It should be pointed out that the easiest course for Republican County Chairman Bulen to have pursued, if he were concerned only about himself and his personal ambitions, would have been to seek party endorsement of Alex Clark or Judge Sharp, both of whom were well known within the organization. But it was the future of his community, his nation, and his party that were foremost in Bulen's mind in the spring of 1967. And he was convinced that the future of Indianapolis would be more secure and more promising under the leadership of Dick Lugar, who would prove that Republicans can administer government best. At a time when other large cities were dying, Bulen wanted to insure a long prosperous life for the city of Indianapolis. He wanted new industry and better jobs for the people living in his city. He wanted to better the aesthetic values of the community, and he wanted sane and sensible fiscal government. Keith Bulen had the courage to promote the man who held forth the promise of realizing those dreams, and with such a man he had two legs of that three legged stool. He had an outstanding candidate, if he could get him nominated, and he had an outstanding political organization, if he could hold it together through the primary election. Money, the third leg, was to remain a serious problem throughout the campaign.

Lugar was young, honest, intelligent, sincere, energetic, had charisma, and was fully aware of the problems facing Indianapolis in the late 1960's. He was a successful businessman and a dedicated public servant who wanted to move the city ahead, instead of accepting the decay facing other cities.

All cities in the state of Indiana were creatures of the state Legislature, and could perform only those functions that the General Assembly allowed them to perform. But Dick Lugar advocated "home rule" for the city of Indianapolis. He promised to lobby hard in the 1969 session of the state legislature for the right of people of his city to govern themselves at the local level. Home Rule was a good issue and Lugar spoke to it with conviction. Candidate Lugar spoke of making Indianapolis a model city, and he spoke of the needs of the people for better services from their government. He was a candidate with all of the positive assets that a party leader could ask for. His intelligence dictated to him that he should listen to, rely upon, and trust the advice and political expertise of his county chairman, as well as the few advisors that Bulen had assembled as a campaign executive committee. That Lugar-Bulen team, their tactics and their results, have become a primer for other candidates and campaign managers throughout the nation.

The people of Indianapolis were witness to a spirited primary election campaign through March and April of 1967. The Lugar-Clark Republican battle was a highly contested affair. Both were running hard, appearing wherever one or more Republicans might assemble, to shake hands and solicit votes. Neither spoke evil of the other and both were dedicated to supporting the victor. The Democratic primary saw the incumbent mayor being challenged by the Democratic county chairman and both Democrats had plenty of evil to espouse about the other.

Before dawn on May 2, 1967, the Republican campaign workers were at the polling places. The precinct committeemen had their supplies, including the slates promoting Dick Lugar and the official Republican team. Bulen had spoken with the precinct committeemen and ward chairmen, and had encouraged them to work as a team, convinced that Lugar could win in the fall. The question arose again, could Bulen hold his team together and inspire them to match their successes of the previous year?

Election day is a hard day for a candidate and his campaign manager. They have done all that they can do at that point. As they wait for the vote to come in, they inevitably recall a few mistakes they should not have made or they remember what they could have done but didn't. But it's too late. On that primary day in May, Lugar visited the polling places seeking last minute votes, as Bulen remained in his office in radio contact with Republican workers, directing the last day of the primary campaign. At approximately 10:00 AM, a report came in that a voting machine had broken down and that Lugar was doing well in that precinct. From that point, the excitement and anticipation of victory began to rise. A few hours later another machine malfunctioned and the machine counter indicated that Lugar was leading Clark. After the polls closed and the returns began coming in, jubilation reigned at Republican headquarters. The final vote revealed that 21,551 Republican voters had pulled Lugar's lever, whereas Clark had garnered an even 17,000 votes. Richard G. Lugar was the Republican nominee for mayor of Indianapolis. Keith Bulen had led his Republican organization through a difficult but highly successful period. It was the second straight year that the Bulen organization had nominated all of the candidates that it had recommended.

In a statement to the organization, Bulen said:

> First, a hearty and genuine thanks to the many, many of you who worked so diligently to achieve the nomination of Dick Lugar in the May 2 primary. You rightfully deserve to be proud of yourselves. The organization withstood a formidable challenge by an extremely popular Republican who waged a vigorous campaign. I know many had mixed emotions concerning the respective candidates; however, most of you stood by the organization and held your ground, and did the job. God bless you.
>
> It is no fun in a Primary for any of us, but it is a necessary part of our political elective processes, and we must face it with honesty and with deep sense of responsibility. The primary contest should prove to us what can be done if we have the courage to stand together. The contest also caused Dick Lugar to campaign vigorously and prove to all that he can and will go all-out in the ensuing months in an effort to be victorious on November 7th. He is campaigning, as he promised, every day and night, and will continue to do so. He is most co-operative and is available to meet with groups or individuals where it can assist us in attracting support for the fall.

Dick Lugar, showing a great deal of maturity as a candidate, gave the following message to Republican workers:

> One of the most important lessons we have learned from our recent Republican mayoralty primary election is the certainty that we can conduct a spirited and hard fought contest without damage to our Party or to the Party's candidates. We were able

to disagree on the objective facts of which candidates for Mayor, City Clerk, and City Council would be the strongest contenders in November and which would best serve Indianapolis with imaginative planning and administrative ability .

I am grateful to all who supported me, but I am also grateful to those who supported Alex Clark and waged a vigorous and resourceful campaign in his behalf. The Republican Party in Indianapolis is stronger because of the skills we have sharpened as workers heavily involved in constructive issues and skilled promotion. I am appreciative especially, for the many acts of encouragement and genuine sportsmanship which characterized the aftermath of the primary election.

The General Election campaign began on May 3. I am pleased that so many Republicans have taken to heart the need to work without pause through November, if we are to maintain a good chance to win. The temptation is great to assume that six months is enough time to work miracles, but we are already hard pressed for time. We must know clearly the ways and means of solving the problems of our city. This will require teams of Republicans involved in research and the stewardship of many Republicans who have planned to give us assistance when we form a new administration in January of 1968.

We know that we will need adequate financial support for the General Election and that a cash flow must be evident throughout the entire six months in order that we may use our resources most efficiently. We know that personal contact with many thousands of voters is essential in the next six months. For this reason, I have tried to accelerate the number of personal appearances which I can squeeze into each day of May and June and to make certain that we are visiting each neighborhood of our city with frequency.

Each day I am more certain that a majority of persons in Indianapolis truly love this city and want a change of direction toward more efficient service and basic trust in the talent and honesty of elected officials. I am grateful that our great Republican organization in Marion County stands for providing the

best candidates, service, and information to the people of India-
napolis. All of my efforts in the field are being supported at head-
quarters in a spirit of complete trust and confidence. I pledge to
think carefully about how each day can be spent most effectively
and to enlist the counsel of others who have already been so help-
ful and will do even more in the weeks to come. This is the great-
est of all years to be the Republican nominee for mayor of In-
dianapolis. At the same time that I say a heartfelt "thank you"
for giving me this opportunity, I am asking each Republican to
do all that he can NOW to insure that our campaign brings not
only a Party victory, but an outstanding milestone in good gov-
ernment, for Indianapolis.

And so, as summer approached, Dick Lugar, Keith Bulen and
the Republican Party in Indianapolis, faced their greatest challenge—
a challenge of doing what could not be accomplished in the past six-
teen years, elect a Republican mayor in the city of Indianapolis.

---

1. Rex Early later served as the Chairman of the Indiana Republican Party.
2. John Sweezy succeeded Bulen as Chairman of the Marion County Republican
   Party.

Chapter Four

As in professional athletics, a championship team needs a real challenge before it performs at its utmost ability. The Marion County Republican Party had the winning spirit, and the organization considered themselves to be of championship caliber. The challenge was awesome—make Indianapolis a Republican city. The Marion County G.O.P. quarterback, L. Keith Bulen, was ready to begin the campaign. He had a winning team with but one weakness. In every campaign, early money is extremely significant. To plan the fall campaign, a campaign manager needs money in the bank and a sufficient projected cash flow to enable him to commit to future expenses. But the money was not easily accessible. Again, having been involved in competitive athletics, Bulen knew that if the team had a weakness, it must be compensated for with other existing strengths. If, in baseball, you have one weak outfielder, you edge the other two strong outfielders closer to the weaker one to help him cover his area. Therefore, Bulen decided the only way to compensate for the lack of finances was to use his organizational and volunteer manpower wisely.

He established a neighborhood issues committee, under the direction of John W. Sweezy. That committee of many, many volunteers spent the summer researching Indianapolis neighborhoods. Young men and women interested in their city and sharing the future hope that Dick Lugar projected, drove their automobiles throughout the various neighborhoods of Indianapolis. They took pictures of crumbling curbs and decaying sidewalks, of chuckholes, and they noted poorly lighted streets. They interviewed the residents to find out what was wrong in the neighborhood that the city government could and should cure. These volunteer investigators discovered an area where there was no sidewalk and children had to walk in a busy street to reach their elementary school. They discovered teenage hangouts which disrupted the peace of the area on weekend nights. They found dirty and poorly marked streets, and alleys littered with trash accumulated over the years. They discovered poor police and citizen relationships in some areas, and they turned up many other problems. The precinct committeemen were also making lists of existing problems in their own precincts.

All of that accumulated information came in to Sweezy and the Neighborhood Issues Committee to be screened and recorded. Armed with such information, the committee drafted individualized personal letters to be sent into the different neighborhoods over Dick Lugar's signature. Those letters said, in effect, that Lugar was aware of the existing problem in each neighborhood, and that if elected as mayor he would attempt to resolve the problem. To each letter he added an appeal for the recipients vote.

The timing was such that the letters were put in the mail so they would arrive just a few days before the election, not allowing the opposition time to respond. The results were better than could have been hoped for. In that age, the average voter became acquainted with candidates mostly through the news media. Few individuals had the opportunity to talk with, or receive a personal letter from, a candidate. And to receive a personal letter from a candidate for major office who was aware of, and promised to correct, a localized problem was also highly unusual, and it proved to be an effective campaign tool.

The incumbent mayor, whose slogan claimed that he "gets things done," was challenged on his failure to solve the problems of the people and the people responded by retiring him. The neighborhood letter campaign was probably the most significant tactic in the 1967 Lugar for Mayor Campaign. Although some may have considered it basic politics, it was a stroke of genius on Bulen's part.

Before each letter was mailed, the members of the Neighborhood Issues Committee rechecked the area to make sure that the problem still existed. Such is the nature of Bulen's mind, to leave no detail unattended. Following his election, Dick Lugar made good on the promises made in those campaign letters. One such promise to the people of the South West Side of Indianapolis was that he would close down an open dump that had been burning and smoldering for years. That open dump had been polluting the air and creating a stench which caused a very unpleasant life for the residents of the area. Immediately after taking the oath of office on January 1, 1968, Mayor Lugar drove to that open dump and officially closed it down, knowing that the future of his city depended upon maintaining the proper ecological balance. A few years before it became fashionable, Dick Lugar was not just talking about pollution, he was arresting it. He was also keeping his campaign promises.

There were twenty other volunteer task forces created during the summer of 1967. The purpose of each was to discover and research the various problems facing the city, and to come up with recommended solutions. The result of those task forces not only made good campaign ammunition, but they were put into practice when Lugar took office. Many highly qualified professional and technical people gave the campaign many man and woman hours, and the needed ability and expertise to get the job done. Armed with the facts accumulated by the task forces, Lugar made the incumbent mayor defend his record by stating the incumbent's failure to act and by offering reasonable solutions. Lugar referred to the incumbent as indecisive and he had the facts to prove it.

Lugar promised in 1967 to make Indianapolis a model city, to rid the taxpayer of the cost of overlapping agencies and responsibilities within the government. The facts and recommended solution in that area were developed by the Home Rule and Metropolitan Government Task Force. Mark W. Murphy directed the activities of the task force, whose members encompassed the best legal and governmental talent in the city of Indianapolis. Even though Lugar and Bulen were directly involved in the progress of each task force, they were especially attentive to the Home Rule and Metropolitan Government Task Force. The reason was simple, if victorious Lugar would use the results of this committee to make Indianapolis a model city, a model not just to set an example for other cities, but to give the people of Indianapolis the best governmental service for the lowest possible cost. It would make the industrial climate of the city such that new jobs would be created and new peoples enticed to move to, and live in, the model city of Indianapolis.

The term "home rule," of course, simply means that the local unit of government is allowed to govern its own affairs. But one of the first observations of the task force was that Indiana was not a home rule state. As previously mentioned, cities in the state of Indiana have only such powers as are granted to them by the Indiana General Assembly.

The term "metropolitan government" in its broadest sense, implies the existence of a single unit of local government with territorial competence over the whole metropolitan area. In Marion County, Indiana, there existed in 1967 many local units of government. There were several cities and towns other than Indianapolis, and there was the county government, which often duplicated or conflicted with city governments. Also, there were other agencies of the city government causing conflicts, such as the Parks Board, whose authority and taxing power were county-wide, although many citizens had no voice in the selection of the administrators of such agencies. The result? Taxation without representation. It was such inefficiency that Lugar spoke of and promised to correct if elected, and if he could convince the 1969 State Legislature to enact enabling legislation.

The results of the Home Rule and Metropolitan Government Task Force, the various attorneys who drafted and perfected the legislation, and the perseverance of Dick Lugar and Keith Bulen with the State Legislators, are now history. Unified Government (Uni-Gov) became reality in Indianapolis, and city leaders from throughout the world were soon traveling to Indianapolis to witness and learn about this revolutionary concept of unified government. For the people of the city, services had been increased as the civil city tax rate was reduced in 1969, 1970, 1971, and 1972.

Other campaign task forces concerned themselves with police services, police morale and recruitment, with municipal code recodification, with human and social relations, with the non-statutory power of the mayor, with traffic flow, parking, and traffic safety, with mass transportation, with street services, curbs, and snow removal, with garbage and refuse disposal, and with citizen involvement in government. William I. Spencer coordinated the entire task force program for the campaign. With the information gained from volunteer task force committees, and the expertise of the various members, channeled in the direction of good government, the Republican

Party not only had the best informed candidates to put before the electorate, but Dick Lugar had a blueprint for a progressive city government that would be responsive to the needs of the people.

Although the campaign was under-financed, there was still a need for paid political advertising. The problem was how could you get the most exposure for your money? Historically, political advertising had been relatively mediocre, but Bulen did nothing in a mediocre fashion. Having an intelligent and saleable candidate was a tremendous benefit. One-half hour television segments were purchased, with Lugar going on live to discuss the problems of Indianapolis. His sincerity and honesty projected through the television screen and into the homes of Indianapolis residents. There was no political double talk, just a frank discussion of the issues.

There was also a need to put something in the hands of the voters, telling them about Dick Lugar and his program. The electronic media could not accomplish that feat, nor could the candidates and volunteers pass out enough handouts to all of the city's voters. In 1966, Bulen had mailed out a highly professional, full color, brochure. Inserted in the brochure was a phonograph recording with messages by Richard Nixon, George Romney, Everett Dirksen, and Dwight Eisenhower. Bulen wanted to do even better in 1967.

Once again he decided upon a full color brochure, this time magazine-size. It was inserted and distributed in an Indianapolis newspaper and reached nearly every voter in the city. It was a twelve page publication, entitled "Forward Indianapolis," and told the detailed Lugar story. It was distributed on Monday afternoon when no other supplements would be in the paper. It attracted much attention, and for several days it remained in places of prominence in many city homes.

Early in the year Bulen asked Gordon Durnil to stockpile hundreds of press releases to be ready to release to the various media each morning and afternoon throughout the campaign. It's not unusual for candidates to not know what they say in a press release until they read it in the paper the next day, because they do not take the time to proofread what the public relations committee writes. Not so with Dick Lugar. He read and reread every release, made deletions, additions and corrections. He scrapped many and wrote many others himself. He was very much concerned with being sincere in his campaign.

At least one public relations gimmick was tried in 1967. A musical jingle, to be played on radio, was devised with a sexy female voice extolling the lyrics of "Dick Lugar, he's first rate. Dick Lugar for a town that's great." One of the truly amusing aspects of the under financed mayoralty campaign was Keith Bulen, who had musical talent, singing words scratched out by Robert Beckman and his wife, while Durnil, Spencer, Sweezy and Bill Colbert, all who were at best tone deaf, passed judgment.

Organized labor had been an area where Republicans traditionally could make little headway, and some party leaders had quit trying. But such were the challenges that Bulen thrived upon. He organized and assembled a twenty-five-member Republican Labor Advisory Committee, the membership of which represented thirteen International unions. The statement of policy formulated by the committee contained five points:

1. To counteract the false image that the Republican Party is anti-labor and the party of the rich.
2. To advise G.O.P. candidates about the needs of working people, union members or not.
3. To recruit and encourage those in the ranks of organized labor toward the philosophies and principles of the Republican Party.
4. To inform working people that the G0P is concerned about them and seek their support.
5. To help legislators draft proper labor legislation and to publicly support Republican candidates.

Young people were working in the Lugar campaign, but wanting more participation from youth, especially with a candidate such as Dick Lugar with whom young people could easily relate, Bulen revitalized the Teen Age Republican Clubs (TARs), and he put them to work on the Lugar campaign.

During the Presidential campaigns of Dwight Eisenhower, a Block Captain system had been used. It was the purpose of that system to divide precincts into city blocks, and to name a captain for each block. The goal was to have an official campaign representative in each city block for the Republican Party. Pulling out all stops and leaving no stone unturned, Bulen reorganized the Block Captain system in Indianapolis to better tell the Lugar Story and to execute the campaign plan.

The Republican organization concentrated on the nuts and bolts of the campaign. The first need was to make sure that every potential Lugar voter was properly registered to vote. Another essential function was for each precinct committeeman to take an accurate poll of his precinct, so that every Republican and Independent voter was known. The poll cards revealed the voters' party affiliation, whether or not he or she needed an absentee ballot, a ride to the polls on election day, had a child in the armed services or college, along with other pertinent information. A get-out-the-vote program was established to guarantee that every potential Lugar voter would cast his ballot. In June, Bulen and John Rowe, city chairman in 1967 and later on the staff of the Republican National Committee, attended a National Committee Campaign School, to make sure that they were not omitting any useful campaign tactic in the Indianapolis mayoralty campaign.

The Greater Indianapolis Republican Finance Committee (GIRFCO) had been formed to provide fund raising for the party on a year around basis. Under the direction of George Tintera, the Neighborhood Finance Committee, a branch of GIRFCO, fielded a volunteer team of thousands who would knock on doors to ask for contributions to the Republican Party. In 1967 the effort was a tremendous success. In fact, the Marion County Neighborhood Finance Committee raised more money each year than did any other similar Republican program in the nation. In the neighborhood program, each township had a finance chairman as did each ward and precinct. Other functions of Greater Indianapolis Republican Finance were sustained giving programs, fund raising dinners, special gifts, etc. As a result, Republican fund raising in Indianapolis was placed on a professional and permanent basis.

The summer of 1967 was a busy time for Indianapolis Republicans. They were so enthused with Dick Lugar and with their own desire to win, that they had forgotten that the odds were against them. An "Elephantorial" in the September, 1967 issue of *The Republican Reporter* reflected that mood and desire. It was entitled "Summer's End."

> *All too soon summer has again passed us by. Leaves of green will soon be brown and the lawnmower will soon lose its place of importance in the garage, to be replaced by the rake, and soon thereafter by the snow shovel. Throughout the warm months since May we have mixed our daily chores with pleasure, spent a few afternoons on the golf course, taken our vacations, and enjoyed the out-of-doors. Unlike the ant and squirrel, who work so hard during the summer accumulating their stores for the winter, we humans like to take it easy during nicer weather.*
>
> *There are many among us who cannot relax at any time throughout the year. Included among that breed are political candidates who must "make all the hay" possible between May and November. The same should be true for those of us who work toward the election of our candidates. For the next two months, it MUST be true, if we have aspirations for success.*
>
> *The summer months of 1967 have found Dick Lugar hard at work not only attempting to win votes, but to prepare himself properly for the task ahead after he wins the election. While others were playing golf, Dick was attending lengthy strategy meetings. While others were enjoying the cool nights in their lawn chairs, Dick was speaking at community meetings. While some were bowling in summer leagues, Dick was running from one bowling alley to another introducing himself to the bowlers. While many of us attended Sunday afternoon picnics in the park, Dick was there introducing himself to the picnickers and promoting the Republican message.*
>
> *Dick Lugar has done, and will continue to do, more than a political party could possibly expect from one of its candidates. We should, at this point, commend Dick's family for sacrificing him to us not only this summer, but the summer of 1966 when*

he so diligently worked on the Congressional campaign. Dick Lugar is an example of how, by sticking together and working for each other, we can make this a Republican city, state and nation.

As November 7, 1967 dawned, and the polls opened, Indianapolis voters could look back and reflect upon the campaign that had commenced in earnest the preceding May. The Democrat organization, aided by 5,000 patronage workers, had waged a tough battle. Their opponents, the Republican organization, had relied on volunteers to stuff envelopes, young people to canvass neighborhoods, and average people willing to take a day off work to be at the polling places to promote Lugar and to insure an honest vote. All varieties of Indianapolis and Marion County residents who simply cared about good government had contributed their time, talents, and money. Also, during those six months, Dick Lugar had been everywhere and had done everything possible to garner votes.

When the polls closed the results were 72,278 votes for Lugar and 63,284 for his opponent.

Lugar, Bulen and the Marion County Republican team had done the impossible. They had elected only the third Republican mayor in forty years. Republicans by the thousands congregated on downtown Indianapolis, and one of the city's most jubilant celebrations got under way. Dick Lugar had received the largest number of votes ever cast for a Republican in an Indianapolis election.

The architect of the Lugar victory, L. Keith Bulen, gave congratulations to his organization which was now being acclaimed in the press as possibly the greatest big city G.O.P. organization in the country:

It was a historic day in the Republican local picture when Dick Lugar became the third Republican Mayor in over forty years.

I know you all were proud of your part in bringing it about. Although it was a very complex campaign, consisting of dozens of different facets, it still was significant to me that when we are united, co-operative, enthusiastic, dedicated and not afraid to work, we can win against great odds. It goes without saying that you must have great candidates, which we had, with Lugar and team. I naturally hope you will enjoy these moments fully, but I can't help but caution that we are only part-way there, as long as the Democrats control the state and national capitols. Many, many, of the Democrat crossovers of this election will return to their Party alignment in 1968, when local specific problems are not as apparent. We had things going for us that probably won't be present next year, but we have also gained a good base from which to build a great organization, capable of doing the job. Take nothing for granted in 1968, or it could be fatal.

It is truly an honor for me to share these eventful, thrilling and victorious years with a great Republican team, composed of you—the honorable and dedicated people who care enough about your government to make the sacrifice involved.

Even after accomplishing the impossible, it was not the past that Bulen was considering. His mind was already planning for the future —for the next election. Electing a Republican as mayor of Indianapolis was not enough for the master politician, he wanted a Republican governor in the State House and a Republican President in the White House. Such was the challenge of 1968 for Keith Bulen.

Chapter Five

Even before the old year of 1967 expired, Bulen was contacted by the leadership of the Nixon for President forces. He, Orvas Beers, an attorney and Republican County Chairman from Fort Wayne, Indiana, along with two state office holders, John Snyder and Edgar Whitcomb,[1] met with the future President to discuss the 1968 campaign in Indiana. Shortly thereafter, Bulen was named by Nixon as his top official representative in the State of Indiana for the 1968 campaign. A few weeks later Bulen and Gordon Durnil met for a late evening dinner to formulate plans for the Indiana Nixon For President Committee. So, as 1967 passed and the new year of 1968 entered, many detailed plans had already been made for the 1968 election, which was to be one of the most exciting in Hoosier political history.

But there was one lingering detail from 1967 to be dealt with before entering into the 1968 campaign. Since Indianapolis was the only major city in the United States to elect a Republican mayor in 1967, the inauguration of Mayor Richard G. Lugar was to be a celebrated event. The first weekend of January, 1968 was inaugural weekend in Indianapolis. A gala inaugural ball was held on the first night, featuring two ballrooms and two orchestras. Both halls were filled to overflowing with jubilant Republicans. The following evening saw the official swearing-in ceremonies at Clowes Hall at Butler University in Indianapolis.

The successes of the past two years inspired the Marion County Republican Organization. The taste of victory was so sweet they wanted more. The organizational confidence was such that there seemed to be little reason why they could not elect the county ticket, the state ticket, and give Richard Nixon the support he needed to be nominated and elected. But Bulen was a realist and a hard taskmaster. He warned of overconfidence, stressed the need for outstanding candidates, and preached the ever-important necessity for the nuts and bolts grass roots work by the organization.

Bulen's prime concern, as always, was his local ticket. There were still a few Democrat county office holders left over from 1964. Nineteen sixty-eight was the year to replace them. Up for election were two judges, the county treasurer, two county commissioners, the county coroner, and county surveyor. Also on the ticket were six state senators and fifteen state representatives. All were extremely important offices in fact, but offices that incite little excitement for the electorate. For that reason Bulen needed someone to lead the ticket. Someone who could excite the voters in November of 1968. Dick Nixon was the one.

Another office up for election in 1968 was the 11th District Congressional seat. It was a district primarily concentrated in the inner city, and it was a paradise for Democrats. No matter how good the Republican candidate (Bulen fielded three outstanding candidates in a row), and no matter how much effort was expended, Democrat Andy Jacobs continued to win the 11th Congressional District of Indiana. This was a situation that Bulen resolved to correct and by a concentrated effort in the 1971 General Assembly a new congressional map was drawn, giving the Republican Party a shot at the eleventh district.

The importance of the state legislative offices in 1968 was obvious. Marion County had eight of the fifty state senators and fifteen of the one hundred state representatives. The determining factor of which party, Republican or Democrat, had a majority in the state legislature, usually depended upon which party won Marion County. Again Bulen went to the screening committee concept to select the best qualified candidates to recommend to the voters. Once again the screening committee did its job well. Each and every one of the screening committee recommendations were nominated and elected.

With their energies now directed in three directions—local, state, and national—the Bulen team was becoming diversified. In 1967 the whole team concentrated upon the one city election. Now some of Bulen's aides were working full time on the Nixon campaign, and others were concentrating on the races for governor and U. S. Senator. Therefore, in 1968, the question was not whether or not the organization could perform, but could it perform as well in so many different areas of concern?

The Republican Party was becoming the "in" party in Marion County. Two consecutive victories for Bulen drew attention to him, and that attention brought various attempts at criticism and even slander. The opposition, not able to beat him at the polls, decided to attack his personal life. As a result Keith Bulen had no real personal life. He gave his life to the party. His goals were success for the party and good government for his fellow citizens. If he had to take abuse to achieve those goals, he would take it.

During this time a placard was hung on his wall—a quote by Abraham Lincoln:

> *If I were to try to read, much less answer, all the attacks made on me, this shop might as well be closed for any other business. I do the very best I know how—the very best I can; and I mean to keep doing so until the end. If the end brings me out all right, what is said against me won't amount to anything. If the end brings me out wrong, ten angels swearing I was right would make no difference.*

Indiana was an important state for Richard Nixon in 1968. He was already the holder of the Indiana primary election plurality record. In 1960 he received over 400,000 votes in the Indiana Presidential Primary. As the 1968 primary approached, with Nixon unopposed, the national media was opining that Nixon should poll more than his record 400,000 votes for the Indiana primary election to be considered a success. Indiana Republicans knew that such a task was nearly impossible in a non-contested race, and even though they publicly stated they were not shooting for the record, they set out to beat it.

The Nixon campaign leadership needed to prove that their candidate was a winner and the primary elections were the places to do it. Candidate Nixon had won several primaries in smaller states before the May 7th primary in Indiana, but Indiana was to be the true proving grounds, the election victory that would catapult Dick Nixon to a successful nomination at the Republican National Convention in Miami.

Bulen organized the Indiana Nixon for President Committee with Orvas E. Beers as chairman. All six Hoosier Republican Congressman, who were seeking re-election, served as honorary co-chairmen. Kurt F. Pantzer, Sr., a prominent Indianapolis attorney and philanthropist, served as treasurer and fund raiser. Gordon K. Durnil was named as the full time executive secretary of the committee. The vice chairlady, Phyllis Gregory, represented northern Indiana, and the secretary was from southern Indiana. A spacious headquarters was opened across Washington Street from the statehouse, and the drive to seek 5,500 names petitioning the Secretary of State to place the name of Richard M. Nixon on the Republican Presidential primary ballot began. Over 30,000 names were secured in a well organized effort. To supplement the political organization of the Indiana Nixon Committee, the Indiana Volunteers For Nixon were organized under the leadership of Charles Shearer.

Bulen requested an early appearance by the candidate and on February 10, 1968, Richard Nixon appeared before a crowd of 9,000 in the southern Indiana town of Washington. A contingent of several hundred Marion County Republicans traveled by chartered bus to meet the former Vice President. It was evident from the reception that Nixon was extremely popular in the state of his mother's birth. He had been in Indiana many times before, as candidate and as citizen campaigning for other Hoosier Republicans. But the Hoosier Nixon leadership knew that popularity and enthusiasm were not enough to equal Nixon's 1960 showing. Good planning and hard work would be required.

On the other side of the political fence, in the Democrat primary, a hot contest was brewing. Scheduled for their first head-on primary battle were Senator Robert F. Kennedy and Senator Eugene J. McCarthy. Also in the battle was Indiana Governor Roger D. Branigin, originally a stand-in candidate for President Lyndon D. Johnson before President Johnson withdrew from the race during the heat of antiwar protests. The Democrat primary attracted many of the national news media, and about one half of the long haired youth in the country. The Republican primary, meanwhile, drew little notice. The Democrat candidates were attempting to stir a large vote and they appealed to Republicans to crossover and vote in the Democrat primary, a procedure that was illegal in Indiana but without penalty. So while Democrat voters were excited and anxious to vote, the Republican voters knew that Nixon would win and saw little reason to bother to cast their vote. Apathy was the opposition for Bulen and the Indiana Nixon Committee. A comprehensive get-out-the-vote effort was needed.

An extensive telephone campaign was organized with a goal of reaching every Republican home in the state of Indiana, encouraging the residents to be sure to vote for Dick Nixon. The calls were made on the Tuesday, Wednesday, Thursday, Friday, Saturday, and Monday, prior to the Tuesday election. There were four shifts of volunteer callers each day, and all calls were live—no recordings. There were over thirty telephone "shops" set up throughout the state, the largest in the Indianapolis Nixon Headquarters, where one hundred and fifty telephones were installed. Each shift of volunteers required 150 callers, supervisory personnel, and a shift of baby-sitters. In the Indianapolis location alone, over 110,000 telephone calls were completed, and on a statewide basis the telephone campaign reached over eighty percent of the Republican homes.

In the midst of the telephone campaign, Richard Nixon made his second appearance of the year in Indiana, this time for a two day tour on May 2nd and 3rd. He appeared in Gary, Indianapolis, Fort Wayne and Evansville. His reception was fantastic at each stop, especially in Indianapolis. If crowd enthusiasm was any indication of success, Nixon certainly appeared to be a big winner in Indiana.

The efforts of Bulen's planning and the co-operative efforts of the Republican leadership throughout the state paid high dividends. Richard M. Nixon received 508,362 votes, and beat his old record by over 100,000 votes. He also received 200,000 more votes than did Senator Kennedy, and 300,000 more than Senator McCarthy. The huge Nixon victory in Indiana proved to be the catalyst needed for his nomination and the Bulen team had again proven their worth.

The next important rung on the 1968 political ladder was the Republican State Convention. Offices up for nomination were U. S. Senator, Governor, Lieutenant Governor, Secretary of State, State Auditor, State Treasurer, Attorney General, Superintendent of Public Instruction, and the State Supreme and Appellate Court judicial candidates. Also to be selected at the state convention would be the twenty-six delegates to the 1968 Republican National Convention. The state convention was set for June 18th, just five days after an appearance in Indianapolis by California Governor Ronald Reagan, himself a potential Presidential candidate.

Indiana was often criticized for continuing the convention system for major office nominations, in lieu of the direct primary concept. However, the Indiana convention was a truly democratic process. There was one delegate for every 400 Republican voters, and those voters, in their own neighborhoods, elected the state convention delegates in their party's primary election. Each delegate had one vote at the convention, whether from a large or small county. The population of each party was equally represented in the Indiana political conventions.

Indiana, being a highly organized state politically, usually nominated good candidates in convention, Republican and Democrat, to oppose each other in the fall. Coalitions could be formed, of course, among like-minded leaders based upon ideals, philosophy, geography, and other criteria. To form an effective coalition with enough votes to effectuate a nomination, however, required a leader able to put all the pieces together. In 1968, L. Keith Bulen was that leader in the state of Indiana.

There were 2,224 delegates to the 1968 Republican State Convention, requiring a nominee to garner 1,113 votes. With a close relationship existing between Marion County with Bulen as Chairman (346 delegates), and Allen County with Orvas Beers as Chairman (119 delegates), forty one percent of the votes needed for nomination were led by two county chairmen. Bulen forged a coalition of large county chairmen (and some small) who represented well over fifty percent of the delegate vote. In return for joining the coalition, many of the chairmen from larger counties were assigned an office up for nomination. Beers supported Bill Salin for Secretary of State and the rest of the coalition chimed in with their support. Bulen supported Bill Ruckelshaus for U.S. Senate and the others did likewise. That pattern followed for all of the offices. The Bulen-Beers team was an effective and responsible coalition for the Republican Party in the state of Indiana, and they, along with other county leaders who joined with them, were one hundred percent effective at the state convention.

Bulen fielded a competent team of Marion County workers to promote the candidates and to pre-count the votes. Each district, and each major county, had a Marion County worker assigned to it by Bulen, and at the final meeting of the team at 2:00 a.m. on the morning of the convention, Bulen's team had determined which counties needed more work, which delegations were safe, and made an educated guess of what the vote would be later on in the day. The early morning educated guess was extremely close to the actual count, and the Bulen team had now mastered another area of political activity— the nominating convention.

At the State Committee meeting immediately following the state convention, L. Keith Bulen was elected to a four-year term as Republican National Committeeman from Indiana. It was in the July issue of *The Reporter* that the following quote appeared:

> *Keith is a winner, as we in Marion County know. His tools for winning have been honesty, integrity, ability, and the true desire to promote better government.* The Reporter *is sure that his leadership abilities will be felt significantly nationally, as they have been at the county and state levels for the last several years.*

With the state convention behind them, attention next focused on the national convention and the twenty-six Hoosier delegates. Marion County delegates to the national convention were Bulen, Mrs. Nola Allen and Mayor Richard G. Lugar. Mrs. Allen was named to the Rules Committee, and Mayor Lugar to the Resolutions Committee at the Miami convention. Mayor Lugar had been campaigning hard for Nixon throughout the first half of the year, as he would continue to do through November. The mayor also served as the National Mayors for Nixon Committee Chairman. The two men, Dick Nixon and Dick Lugar, had many similarities.[2] Both were intelligent and well qualified for the highest of public offices. Both were calm and methodical in their approach to governmental crisis, and both were sensitive men, with a firm understanding and deep concern for the needs of the people. It was at the convention in August, 1968, where Lugar's abilities first attracted national attention. He arrived in Miami a week early to put into resolution form, for the Republican National Committee, the needs of the American people and the various means by which a Republican President could be responsive to these needs.

Bulen, Beers, and Durnil, also arrived early to coordinate the Hoosier delegation on behalf of Richard Nixon. Again they were successful. All 26 Indiana delegates cast their votes for Richard M. Nixon for nomination as a candidate for President of the United States. Only five states cast more votes for Nixon than Indiana. Orvas Beers, the Indiana Nixon Committee Chairman, served as chairman of the Credentials Committee at the National Convention. And, as the convention adjourned, and Dick Nixon was the Republican Presidential candidate, Indiana Republicans had made an impact and contributed significantly to the President's success in Miami. The political expertise of Keith Bulen, and the competence and leadership ability of Dick Lugar, had also been prominently displayed in national Republican politics.

---

1. Ed Whitcomb later served as Governor of the state of Indiana.
2. Cynics should remember that this passage was written prior to Watergate revelations.

Chapter Six

As Labor Day of 1968 passed, the Hoosier campaign was in full gear. William D. Ruckelshaus, an Indianapolis attorney, was the U.S. Senate candidate and he was making daily political appearances throughout the state. He had previously served as Majority Leader of the Indiana House of Representatives. He had a tough opponent in Senator Birch Bayh, who was seeking a second term. In 1969 Ruckelshaus served the Nixon Administration as Deputy U.S. Attorney General, and in 1970 he became the first Administrator of the U.S. Environmental Protection Agency. The rest of the state candidates were running hard statewide, but they were looking to Marion County to provide a sufficient plurality to offset the Democrat stronghold of Lake County, located in northwestern Indiana near Chicago.

Bulen was directing the Marion County Organization to a third straight win, but in a September message, he warned:

> We are getting a late start this year. This is mostly because of the lateness of the national convention. It is a sobering realization to appreciate the importance of this election to our party, state, and nation, and also realize that we are so far from being prepared. Financially, and in the areas of polling and registration, there is an almost impossible task to be accomplished. We have less than a month for our registration effort, and a week for completion of polling. Because of our enormous state and national assessments, our budget is up well over 250 percent, and much of our organizational talent is being specifically utilized in the campaigns of President, Governor, U. S. Senator and Congressmen. It means the balance of the team must work harder than ever before. We can and we must win this election.
>
> George Wallace is going to get some votes. Let's make sure these votes are not Republican votes. We can not afford to scatter our shots or squander votes when we are the minority party. Indiana has a long way to go on the national political scene, but

we are on our way, and it depends almost wholly on our ability to win this one. Certainly Nixon and his staff feel very warmly toward Hoosiers. To indicate his regard for Indiana, we have received his commitment to appear here on Monument Circle, Thursday, September 12th, at 4:30 p.m., and then he will meet with the national leaders of the Citizens for Nixon-Agnew that same night. There will be leaders here from every state and it is an honor to host this significant conference, not to mention the shot in the arm by the next President's public appearance just a few months after being here for the Southport Rally.

Mayor Lugar has kept the faith by working harder and longer than any mayor in our city's history. His administration has eliminated government jobs, lowered the civil city tax rate while all other major cities are raising taxes. He reduced unemployment as he encouraged and stimulated a major rise in private business investment with the city, etc. etc. etc. These many significant accomplishments in such a short time means that new leadership and new ideas can solve the complex problems of our modern society.

Such new direction can only be supplied by Republicans who are not committed to the ineffective past programs instituted and perpetuated by long entrenched Democrat administrations on the state and national level.

Mayor Lugar also had a September message to the organization. His message dealt with the issue of crime, and offered proof of Republican ability to administer government. His message, in part, read:

We have sought the best quality and quantity of service from our citizens to meet head-on the problems of prejudice, unemployment, housing, youth programs, and respect for law, and a society based on law, which improves as we draft careful and thoughtful plans for improvement. At the same time, we have appointed a Police Chief, Winston L. Churchill, and high ranking officers, who are sensitive to human needs, but true professionals in the best sense of good law enforcement. They have attracted more volunteers for active duty on our police force during the past few months than during any other period since World War II.

Chief Churchill believes we will meet our authorized strength of 1084 men in 1969 for the first time in our history. We started 1968 with fewer than 900 officers. We are dedicated to the proposition that intelligent, vigorous volunteers for police service to our community are making and will make a strong impact in our relentless fight against all forms of crime in this city. We are recognizing individual achievements each month with individual awards and citations. We have asked for compensation increases worth in excess of $500 for each man in the 1969 budget, and for a sharply increased equipment budget to afford a greater option of law enforcement tools to each officer even while reducing the overall civil city property tax rate.

I am grateful that our Party, through its national leaders, Richard M. Nixon, and others, have expressed our idealism clearly and that our local administration has been given the opportunity to prove that this idealism is sound through day-to-day administration of a growing and vital city.

We are a Party of constructive deeds, of promises fulfilled, and of confidence in our Constitutional framework and the opportunities it affords for a just society.

Four o'clock on a Thursday afternoon is a difficult time to attract a crowd for a political speech, even when the speaker is a Presidential candidate. The September 12th Nixon Rally was to be held on the famous Monument Circle, the "hub" of the City of Indianapolis. In such an expansive outdoor area, any crowd of less than 10,000 would appear to be a failure. But the Bulen team had considerable crowd building experience under their belts by this time, and, on September 12, 1968, Presidential Candidate Nixon spoke to a massive crowd of Hoosiers. Bulen, in his excitement, introduced Nixon as "the president of the next United States." Another feature of the Nixon appearance was the Nixon Caravan, from the airport to Monument Circle. The caravan, under the direction of the Marion County

Young Republicans, passed thousands of cheering supporters as it wound its way to the center of the city. In October, Vice Presidential candidate Spiro T. Agnew made an appearance in Indianapolis, and it too was highly successful.

The appearance of the national candidates provided the glamorous aspects of the campaign, but the real organizational effort was being performed at the precinct level. Bulen stressed the need to do all of the "nuts and bolts" activities that his team could do so well.

The results are history. 1968 was a great year for the Republican Party. Marion County more than carried its share of the load, and Keith Bulen and the Marion County Republican team won their third straight election. Indiana gave President Nixon his largest margin of victory of any state in the union. The President received a 499,704 victory in the nationwide popular vote, and 261,226 of that plurality was gained in Indiana. The Indiana Nixon for President effort, under the direction of L. Keith Bulen, had done its job well.

For the first time in eight years, the Governor of the state of Indiana was again a Republican—Edgar D. Whitcomb. All state offices were headed by Republicans. The Republicans had a majority in the State Legislature, and there were no Democrat County or City office holders in Marion County, Indiana. The icing on the cake, was that Richard M. Nixon was now the President of the United States, a Republican. When Keith Bulen was elected County Chairman in 1966, the absolute opposite had been true. The task now was to preserve what had been won.

Chapter Seven

Nineteen sixty-nine was a different kind of year for Marion County Republicans. Following three straight election years, it was a year when there was to be no election. The organization could relax, but for those who had been elected to public office, it was a time to perform. For Bulen, as National Committeeman, it was the first year that he was responsible for all activity in Indiana on behalf of the national party and the new national administration. It was a year when many key members of the political organization were assuming positions in federal, state and local government. This exodus of Marion County talent caused Bulen to worry about his potential for success in the 1970 elections.

The new year was a festive one. On New Years Day, the Marion County Republican officials elected in 1968 were sworn into office in an official ceremony. On January 13th, Governor Edgar D. Whitcomb took the oath of office, followed by a gala inaugural ball held in two locations to accommodate a crowd desiring to celebrate the first Republican governor in the past eight years. The 1969 session of the Indiana General Assembly was in session, and on January 17th, approximately six hundredHoosiers left Indianapolis to participate in the Presidential inauguration of Richard M. Nixon.

As in all of his endeavors, Bulen wanted the Indiana delegation to outshine all others at the Inauguration. A headquarters was established in Washington, D. C., and was manned full time for the entire week under the direction of Nick Longworth. Bulen hosted two receptions, one for Hoosier Congressmen, and one for the new governor. The National Inaugural Committee made several references to the tremendously well organized Indiana delegation, and *The Washington Post* also complimented Indiana on its many activities. The true proof of Hoosier efficiency was the many residents of other states who came to the Indiana headquarters for information.

By February, the final report of the 1968 Neighborhood Finance Committee was ready. By going door-to-door soliciting funds for the

Republican Party, the Marion County Republican "door knockers" had collected more than $90,000.00. The more than 10,000 individual contributions helped the Marion County Republican Committee get out of debt, an unusual situation for any political organization shortly after a major election.

Not all Republicans were happy. There was dissension growing in the ranks. A few egos were bruised. The party now had everything going its own way, with Republicans administering almost every governmental office. Many team members were now looking for the reward that they certainly deserved. The obvious reward would be a position in government, if not for them, then for a friend. In a May, 1969, message, Bulen addressed himself to the problem, in a typically candid manner:

> These are the times that try Republican souls and our solidarity.
>
> The President didn't end the seven year Viet Nam war the day he took office. Democrats are still on the payrolls at all levels and were not all turned out promptly, without qualified replacements. Many of us didn't get, or haven't yet gotten, what we secretly had staked out as our personal, deserved reward. One half of the team is jockeying for control and furthering their personal political ambitions now, instead of waiting until the election year. The self-interest groups are yelling so loudly, because they didn't get their way in the Legislature or Congress, that we are afraid to admit we are Republicans. Republican styled contractors, engineers and vendors haven't gotten rich yet doing business with our various levels of government, and, to top it off, we are stuck with an extra hour of daylight in Indiana and apparently nothing constructive to do with it.
>
> Well—would you believe that the candidates you supported, who are now officeholders, are still better qualified than the Democrats, and are doing a far better job than has ever been done before, and that good, honest government is rarely extremely popular, because too many people get their private playhouses broken up? You can not keep many people happy very long, and

some people never, and it is a lot easier to throw up your hands than it is to keep on trying to straighten things out that are involved and confused.

We can gripe and sit out 1970 on our hands, or we can get up and give administering government our very best efforts to unsnarl the "mess" we won. The officeholders and their staffs sure as the devil can't do it alone, without us, anymore than they could have gotten elected without us, but now many of us stop and leave the whole can of worms for them to unravel. We drop a 15,000 member, vigorous organization here in our county, all working together, suddenly onto a few hundred to do the job. Sure, the job is a different one, but to win an election is only half a loaf, if we don't accomplish meaningful and positive action to meet the complex and constantly changing legion of difficulties facing our city, state and nation.

I am no happier than the unhappiest of you, because I am getting all the complaints of dissatisfaction on all levels of government, now ranging from chuck holes in city streets and dirty toilets at the State Parks, to Red Blount's taking the Post Office Department out of politics. Besides that, both of my personal secretaries are sick, and I can't even get a letter out or a phone call returned. I turned down one of the best appointments in the entire federal government because it was "Hatched," and I would have to give up participation in the Republican Party. It was then and there that I decided I was not going to bug out. Not now, when we are needed the most to support our administration, and if you are half the great gang, that I know you are, you won't "bug out" either.

Organizational pains were not unexpected, especially with a highly competent political organization in a non-election year. Effective leadership can lead an organization successfully through such periods, and Bulen was an effective leader. There were also good things going on that minimized the problem areas. Mayor Lugar was named by the Nixon Administration as a member of the Advisory Commission of Intergovernmental Relations. Keith Bulen was appointed by the Republican National Chairman as a member of the Executive Committee of the Republican National Committee. The Marion County Young Republicans were involved in a paint-up, fix-up, clean-up program in various neighborhoods of the city. Using private donations and volunteer man hours, the Y.R.'s, in their "Upgrade 69" program, helped repair various civic centers, nursing homes, day care centers, and other community facilities.

Even though Republican Headquarters was a beehive of activity, the organization enjoyed a nonpolitical summer. In August, Keith Bulen and Orvas Beers visited with the President, to celebrate the first anniversary of the Nixon Presidential nomination. By fall, however, the planning and fund raising for the 1970 elections were under way. William D. Ruckelshaus, then the Assistant U. S. Attorney General, was scheduled in to speak to a $100 banquet in October. The fund raising banquet was a success, setting a Marion County record for profits.

As the year closed out, Bulen organized an extensive educational seminar for the organization. The seminar was named the Republican College For Political Knowledge, and Bulen set out details of the program in his November message to the organization:

> *Mark Saturday, December 13th, all day, if you are a Marion County Republican Committeeman, Vice Committeeman, Ward Chairman or Vice Ward Chairman. This is the most important political date in 1969 for our organization. On that day, at Clowes Hall, for the first time anywhere, we are going to make our case in depth, informative and documented, in behalf of the national, state, and local Republican administrations. The same case, point by point, that we must take to the voters in 1970, and ask them to re-elect Republicans. Commiserating with our constituents will not carry the day for us in '70, '71 and '72. We must be positively prepared to point to our constructive accomplishments (and they are legion) at all levels, as well as our programs for the future.*
>
> *We are in a different posture than before. We are the ins, not the outs. It is natural to dismiss the accomplishments of our*

Administration and dwell on minor misadventure. This can not and will not happen to us if we go into polling and registration in 1970 fully informed and confident in our approach to the voters, as we deservedly ask for their continued confidence. Tom Perrine and his Blue Ribbon committee have been hard at work for months professionally and elaborately preparing to dramatically and colorfully present to our Marion County Republican Organization the Victory College of Political Knowledge. The State Committee members, and all Indiana county chairmen are invited to attend and observe, as will, be office holders. The National Committee is assisting and observing this as a pilot program with the possibility in mind of a similar prototype for other metropolitan Republican Organizations.

On Friday night, December 12th preceding Saturday's curriculum will be a dinner dance and gala party. This will be our combined Annual Christmas party and Central Committee's "Thank You" to the organization for three years of dedicated, effective, and victorious endeavors.

The College was a great success, and the year ended with the organization primed for the 1970 elections.

In his Christmas message, Bulen expressed his inner feelings to the many workers who had brought outstanding success to the Republican Party in Indianapolis:

I suppose if there is such a thing as editorial license, then for this particular column, I claim it, in behalf of the spirit of this Holiday Season, brotherly love, and well wishing.

Nostalgia is the order of the day in this season. The good and warm memories of the last four years outweigh the bad ones. The friends pale the enemies. The brave stand out above the faint hearted. The good motives overwhelm the selfish. The loyal outnumber the defectors, and our accomplishments loom large on the horizon of government. To look back over our shoulders one brief last time together is human. To see where we were and to see where we have come is rewarding. It was one of life's trips that we shared with many of the finest persons of our times, toward some of the loftier goals that man can pursue.

The literally hundreds of thousands of man hours, dollars, sweat and tears going into "our thing" are immeasurable and the strain and pain are incalculable, as is the effect of our combined efforts upon the direction of our local, state and national governments and their respective destinies. I hope there are none among us who begrudge giving up part of their lives to these activities, or who aren't proud to have played a part in our achievements.

I deeply appreciate the confidence and loyal support you have given me. Any honors that may have come my way are meaningless if you do not share them, for they are, indeed, yours. Although we have had little time these four years to know each other's hearts, I do know this about you—only so long as there remain in our nation those like you who choose to work within the framework of our laws and constitution in order to prove that our form of government can and will work, will our nation in reality continue to be "the land of the free and the home of the brave."

Chapter Eight

Nineteen seventy kicked off with the concept of unified government in Indianapolis and Marion County becoming reality. The concept, and its success, is discussed elsewhere in this book, but it was a monumental event for the residents of the community. As in any effort to effectuate change, there was opposition to unified government. Most of the opposition was voiced by Democrat hopefuls, and as a result, Uni-Gov was to be a campaign issue in 1970 and again in 1971.

On February 5, 1970, Indianapolis was the scene of another first. The President of the United States brought his cabinet and advisors to the people. Mayor Lugar and President Nixon were co-hosts to a meeting of ten mayors from throughout the nation to discuss the problems of urban America. Attending the meeting with the President were the Secretary of Agricultural, the Secretary of the Treasury, the Attorney General, the Secretary of the Interior, the Secretary of H. U. D., the Secretary of Transportation, the Director of O.E.O, as well as several other dignitaries and Presidential advisors. It was truly a historic event for the city of Indianapolis, as it would have been for any city.

Before the turn of the New Year, John K. Snyder, Treasurer of the state of Indiana, announced his intent to seek the Republican nomination for the United States Senate. By January, Bulen and a group of Republican leaders decided to find another candidate for the office. The first of three "secret" meetings were held in Indianapolis in January, the second on February 8th in Fort Wayne, and the third on March 1st in Kokomo, Indiana. Party leaders were welcomed to the secret meeting in Fort Wayne by a hotel sign welcoming Republican leaders. The result of these meetings was the formation of the Republican Open Convention Committee. John Snyder had displayed competence in office, and he was a well known and well liked Hoosier Republican. He also had the support of many state office holders, as well as many of those in state Republican leadership positions. Snyder was a formidable opponent and he would be a hard candidate to beat in the 1970 Republican State Convention. Indiana had not elected a Republican Senator since 1956, and it was the purpose of the Open Convention Committee to come up with a candidate with the best chance of defeating the Democratic incumbent. There were other candidates who could perhaps win in the fall, if they could be nominated in the convention. The Bulen forces were seeking a candidate with not only the proper GOP appeal to be nominated, but one with the best broad-based appeal to enhance his chances of being elected in the fall.

The battleground for this contest to be held at the state convention was twofold. First the favorable delegates had to be elected at the May primary, and secondly, a majority of the delegates must be convinced to vote for the Open Convention Committee candidate at the convention.

The Honorable Charles A. Halleck, a thirty-year Hoosier Congressman was named as Honorary Chairman of the Open Convention Committee. D. Russell Bontrager, a former U.S. Senate nominee became Chairman, with Gordon K. Durnil, as Treasurer. Vice-Chairmen of the committee included Mrs. Nola Allen, Orvas E. Beers, L. Keith Bulen, Robert J. DuComb, Paul H. Green, Virgil D. Scheidt,[1] and George R. Glass, all of whom were Republican district or county chairmen. It was a powerful coalition that Bulen had put together in early 1970.

Congressman Richard L. Roudebush, a five-term member of Congress from Central Indiana, was the Open Convention Committee choice as the U. S. Senate candidate.

The committee members began an extensive evaluation of each of the state's 92 counties, to determine support for or opposition to, Roudebush. In the counties where opposition was found, a separate slate of pro-Roudebush delegates candidates was filed. Numerous receptions were held throughout the state with Roudebush greeting potential delegates and party leaders. An extensive direct-mail campaign on behalf of the candidate was also launched.

As the May 5th primary election approached, Bulen had a well oiled political machine functioning on the state level, but he had not ignored his county ticket. Up for election at the county level were the judicial candidates, the Prosecutor, the County Clerk, the Sheriff, other county offices, and the legislative candidates. Most of these candidates were the same ones who had been elected under Bulen's leadership in 1966. The screening committee selected a few new faces, but the team was mostly incumbents with good records of performance. Bulen chose, as a campaign slogan, "Marion County Republicans Have Done A Good Job." The phrase might seem trite, but it was a good choice. Nineteen-seventy was the year of the undersell, a year that found the voters tired of the shouting and bravado often heard in political campaigns.

A new political committee was formed in Marion County prior to the primary, a committee with the intent to file an anti-Bulen slate of state convention delegate candidates. Under the name of the Republicans for a Free Choice Committee, delegate candidates were solicited and filed to run against those delegates endorsed by the Marion County Republican Central Committee. The Free Choice Committee was attempting to do what the Open Convention Committee was doing in other counties. The Free Choice leadership, however, overlooked the loyalty and trust that Republicans in Marion County had for Keith Bulen. The May 5th primary election was extremely successful for the Bulen team. All slated candidates were nominated easily in Marion County. But the truly fantastic achievement is that out of 424 delegate candidates endorsed by the Marion County Republican Party, 424 were elected. To achieve such an accomplishment without an organized opposition is remarkable, but this one hundred percent success was gained over the efforts of the Free Choice Committee. Elsewhere, throughout the state, in every county where there was confrontation, the pro-Roudebush delegates were the victors.

The next hurdle was the June 18th Republican Convention and once again the Bulen team was ready. With three and one half years of experience under their belts, the Marion County Republican Organization went into action. Bulen established various committees to serve the delegates. There were hospitality room committees, information booth committees, a medical room led by Dr. Dennis Nicholas with doctors and nurses, a safety and security committee, a transportation committee, a communications committee, and a committee to build crowds. The most significant committee was the political activities committee, with Bulen and Durnil as co-chairmen. It was the political activities committee that would pre-count and attempt to garner votes.

John Snyder, being an adept politician, withdrew his candidacy prior to the convention. The generous gesture by Snyder was probably prompted partially by the Roudebush primary delegate victories, but also by his desire for party unity. Snyder was later elected as the State Chairman of the Indiana Republican Party.

There were still battles to be won at the convention. Incumbent Secretary of State William Salin was opposed, and the Bulen coalition had pledged their support for Salin. Also, since Snyder was not seeking re-election as State Treasurer, the race was a wide open, three-man contest. Bulen supported John M. Mutz, a state Representative who had proven himself a highly talented individual in both government and business. There were other offices up for nomination, but all were incumbents, and Bulen pledged not to oppose any Republican incumbent office holder.

Throughout the evening and night preceding the convention, the Political Activities Committee members were doing their job with trained expertise. Several times the committee met to arrive at a projected count. The final count was within a whisker of being right on the nose. The committee missed the Mutz count by only eight votes out of the 2,690 delegates at the convention. The Salin count was also amazingly close to the committee's projection.

As the 1970 State Convention adjourned, Keith Bulen had again won every contest.

In July, the following editorial appeared in *The Republican Reporter*:

> Having just passed through another state convention, and
> having witnessed the multitude of good Republicans who
> worked so hard, and volunteered so much of their time, I again

feel I must reflect upon the why of it all.

Why do housewives sacrifice time from their homes to type and stuff political mailings? Why do professional people forego many of their income producing hours to volunteer their abilities? Why would a man put in a hard day's work at the factory, or wherever he may be employed, and then volunteer to help nominate and elect certain candidates?

Why do our party leaders take on the task of leading our party, knowing that criticism will outweigh compliments? Why do men aspire to the Presidency, with the tremendous burdens of that job?

Good government is the answer, of course, but does that adequately answer the question?

I am sure that a few may enter into political activity with the hope of personal reward. If that is their only goal, then they probably won't be around very long—because the duties, and the responsibility, and the pain, are far more demanding over the years, than any reward can adequately compensate.

We are fortunate, in Indiana, to have men and women leading our party, who seek only the reward of having the opportunity to do their thing—to play a role in the history of their county, state, or nation—to help promote and protect the system that guarantees individual freedom. Men whose reward is seeing the American Flag fluttering in the breeze, and can feel proud of knowing, that in their way, they helped maintain all that our Stars and Stripes represent.

As the housewife watches television, or reads the newspaper, and considers the calm and logical judgment of President Nixon in his quest to end the war and save American lives she can say to herself, I helped elect him in 1968. I played a part.

Hoosiers are proud to be Americans. We love our country, and we have an enviable record in the battles to preserve our way of life since Statehood in 1816. We believe in the right to dissent, but we believe that law-breakers must be punished. We are industrious, we pay our taxes, and we support the government.

In considering the whys of political activity, I always have two thoughts. The first is, if I don't do something, will someone else fill the void, or will the void result in something less than good government? The second is Benjamin Franklin's answer to a question following the Constitutional Convention. He was asked what type of government our founding fathers had given us, and he replied, "A Republic, if you can keep it."

We have kept it for 196 years. We have come to the brink of losing it over the years, but the question remains – can we keep it? If you and I don't try, who will?

We are a government of amateurs. There is no school to train Presidents, governors, or Congressmen. As amateurs, we are not perfect. But then we don't want a perfect government, but a government of the people. It is my opinion that a government of the people is the more perfect government ordained by the Preamble of our Constitution. Our government of the people will make mistakes from time to time. Twelve years of mistakes, however, should be more than Hoosier voters are willing to accept from their United States Senator.

I am glad that patriotism is again in vogue, and I intend to do all I can to elect a United States Senator from Indiana who is a patriot and a man of the people. I sincerely hope most Hoosiers will join the cause in 1970, and elect Roudebush on November 3rd.

Bulen selected Durnil to be the Campaign Coordinator for Congressman Roudebush in the 1970 Indiana U. S. Senate Campaign.

Another unusual event took place in July. Keith Bulen left Indiana for thirty days during an election year. He left the reins of the party in the hands of several of his trusted assistants, and he made frequent transatlantic telephone calls.

His reason for leaving was not questioned because he had been selected as the United States Delegate to the 49th Economic and Social Council of the United Nations, meeting in Geneva, Switzerland. Bulen, who had participated successfully in political affairs at the precinct, township, city, county, state and national levels, now had the opportunity to display his expertise on the international scene. The American Ambassador to ECOSOC, the Honorable Glenn A. Olds, reported that Bulen was as adept at that level, as he had been at all of the others.

Bulen reported, "To have occupied the United States chair during a session of the full plenary that coordinates, directs, or supervises over two-thirds of all United Nations projects, programs, funds and personnel, was the height of fulfilling the great American dream." He also said, "It is no great feat to recognize the actual effect of our political activity in the precincts and counties of Indiana upon the role the United States plays on the international scene."

Upon Bulen's return from international diplomacy, he was ready to return to the Hoosier political wars, and it was in August that the campaign began in earnest.

For Republicans to win a statewide election in Indiana, a large plurality was needed from Marion County. A fifteen-thousand vote plurality in Marion County, coupled with an eight to ten thousand win in Allen County, would normally offset the Democrat strongholds of Lake and St. Joseph counties. But in the 1970 Hoosier U.S. Senate race, the Democrats were pulling out all stops. As previously stated, there were more Democrats in Indiana than there were Republicans. If the Democrats could get out their vote, they would win. In 1970, the Democrats employed an out-of-state consultant, Matt Reese, to get out the Democrat vote.

The Republican campaign had assistance from the national party and the White House. A partial list of those coming to Indiana to assist Roudebush were the President, the First Lady, the President's daughter, the Vice President twice, the Attorney General, the Secretary of H.U.D., the Secretary of Labor, the Republican National Chairman, Presidential counselors, Senators and Congressmen. The mere coordination of those various V.I.P. appearances became a full time campaign responsibility.

The campaign was a difficult one, with a televised debate between the two candidates for U.S. Senate, and a controversy over the fairness of a television commercial. Both candidates made multiple daily campaign appearances. A significant factor in the statewide election was the U.A.W. automotive strike and the downturn of the economy shortly before election day. Both events were damaging to the Republican cause. The results of the U. S. Senate race were a long time coming, and it turned out to be the closest Senate contest in Indiana history.

The Democrat get-out-the-vote campaign had worked well in every large county except Marion (Indianapolis). Under Bulen's leadership, all Marion County Republican candidates were elected easily, and a large plurality was rolled up for the state candidates. It was the first time, in the memory of G.O.P. old-timers, that a Marion County Chairman had won four consecutive elections, as Bulen had done in 1966, 1967, 1968 and 1970.

1. Virgil Scheidt later served as Chairman of the Indiana Republican Party.

Chapter Nine

With the arrival of 1971, Bulen was relishing the upcoming campaign to re-elect Dick Lugar as mayor of Indianapolis. For the first time in his career as party chairman, Bulen was looking at an opportunity to run a technically perfect campaign. Dick Lugar was a near-perfect candidate, with a good record of success as mayor. The Bulen county political organization was probably the best in the country, and financial problems were not as serious as usual. Many people were willing to invest their future, their time, their ability, and their money, in Dick Lugar.

The Indianapolis municipal elections were to be unlike any preceding election. The unified government concept, now in force, called for twenty-five separate councilman districts, with each councilman representing approximately 31,000 residents. Always before the city council candidates had campaigned on a county-wide basis. Added to the twenty-five district candidates, were four at large council seats to be elected by all voters in the county.

The State Legislature began its 93rd session in January. Under a new State Constitutional amendment, the legislature would begin meeting annually instead of the pervious biennial sessions. As a result of the annual sessions, and because of the resignation of a Marion County Representative, the governor called a special election to fill the vacant seat to be held simultaneously with the municipal election. The legislature also created two new Criminal courts for Marion County, with the judges to be elected in 1971. With these additions, thirty-three offices were up for election.

Another first time event of the 1971 elections resulted from unified government in Marion County. All eligible voters in the entire county would have the right to vote for the mayor of Indianapolis, the four at large councilman candidates, and one district candidate. An oddity of the law allowed residents of other cities within the county to vote for two mayors—the mayor of Indianapolis and the mayor of their local municipality. That oddity, and the fact that many suburban voters did not know they were eligible to vote for the Indianapolis mayor, required an educational effort by Bulen, because for Lugar to win, a strong turnout among the suburban voters was necessary.

By the end of three years in office, Lugar had become involved in government at the national and international levels. Indianapolis was the largest city in the nation with a Republican administration, and the national administration had come to rely on Indianapolis and Lugar for leadership in solving the great urban problems of the seventies. As a result of Lugar's national involvement, his concern for, and success in, solving local problems, and his closeness to the people of Indianapolis, his name recognition was nearing the one-hundred percent mark.

One of the key factors that a campaign manager looks for in a candidate is name familiarity among the electorate. But because of the Lugar name recognition, and his favorable performance ratings, Bulen experienced a new problem with Indianapolis Republicans— apathy. As the election year dawned, almost anyone who was asked believed that Lugar would be re-elected easily, and the workers did not feel the challenge to perform in the underdog fashion of previous elections. It was Bulen's job to convince the workers that they had to give their maximum effort in 1971 to get the job done. An average performance would result in a loss.

To firm up the organization, and to make sure every member of the Marion County Republican team knew of the Lugar successes, Bulen held a series of organizational meetings. The first meeting was on January 4, 1971, and the last on January 29th. Each and every precinct committeeman, vice committeeman, ward chairman and vice ward chairman, and Republican office holder, heard Bulen, Mayor Lugar, and the Uni-Gov directors, explain what unified government was, and how it was performing. It was imperative that each member of the organization knew the facts, and that they were all telling the same story to the voters. Imperative because misinformation was rampant regarding Uni-Gov, and some of the problems were festering in Republican ranks.

By January, potential Democrat candidates for mayor were criticizing the new concept of government, now in its second year. Assuming that Democrats would make Uni-Gov an issue, Bulen was dedicated to sharing the facts, pro and con, to the people who would do the campaign work in the precincts. Each would be an ambassador for the mayor in his or her respective neighborhood, and it was important that each person understand what Uni-Gov really was—a concept with flexibility, not perfect, but better than anything from the past.

How government was administered was not normally of concern to voters, providing it was honest, efficient, and responsive. In that first month of 1971, however, suburban voters were concerned about fears formed from misinformation about Uni-Gov. They feared that Uni-Gov would take control of their local school boards, that volunteer fire departments would be demobilized, that township government would be abolished, that their tax rate would go up, that the Sheriff's Department would be abolished, that they would be forced into the Indianapolis Police District, and that their suburban way of life would be drastically changed. None of these fears were based on fact, and by the end of January, the Marion County Republican Organization was armed with the facts to defend and promote the Uni-Gov concept.

Another feature of these organizational meetings, in the first month of the campaign year, was the distribution of priority action forms. These forms were to be used by the precinct committeemen to point out problems in their neighborhoods that could be resolved by city government, and the mayor's office responded to these requests for action. Chuckholes were filled, missing street signs were replaced, crumbling curbs and sidewalks were mended, dirty streets were cleaned, roving dog packs were broken up, traffic lights installed, and various other day to day problems of municipal housekeeping were solved. Although the priority action forms were being dismissed by some as old-time party politics, it was, in fact, a method by which city government became more responsive to the needs and desires of the people. If citizens had complaints, they could go to their neighborhood precinct committeeman for results, instead of to a bureaucracy down at city hall.

Another important decision was made in January, 1971. Lugar's re-election campaign would be well funded. Every element of the Bulen's campaign plan had been costed out and he arrived at a professional budget of $687,292.00. His finance plan indicated that he would have the resources to fund the budget.

The important decisions in most political campaigns are made by the campaign manager. The planning, the rough drafts of proposals and press releases, the ideas, volunteer recruitment, media usage, themes, and almost all relevant plans, are the responsibility of the manager. Often the candidate and a few key lieutenants will participate in the decision-making, but few campaign managers will take the gamble of delegating authority. Campaigns can be won or lost by small decisions as well as large ones. An example is the thousands of letters that a candidate receives during a campaign. Each letter must be answered promptly and correctly. If a letter is not answered, a voter is alienated, but if it is answered with an unsatisfactory form letter, not just the writer is alienated, but so are the writer's friends and neighbors to whom the letter is shown. The voter may even be mad enough to write a letter-to-the-editor of the local newspaper. On the other hand, if a campaign manager reads and answers each and every letter, he has little time for the major decisions of the campaign. If he delegates letter-answering to someone else, he fears the answers will not be drafted correctly, and if he doesn't answer the letters at all, he loses votes. Constituent letters are but one example of small problems turning large—just one example of the campaign manager's all encompassing task. But in Marion County, Indiana, Bulen was not afraid to delegate responsibility to those who had proven themselves in past campaigns. As a result, the Lugar re-election campaign of 1971 would be one of the most diversified in Indiana political history.

To begin his delegation of authority, Bulen called a weekend meeting, on January 23rd and 24th, at French Lick, Indiana. French Lick, a small Southern Indiana community, noted in an earlier time for its medicinal baths, gambling, and political gatherings, had been the kicking off point for many Hoosier political campaigns. It was in this quaint setting that Bulen made campaign assignments—not mere paper titles, but real jobs to dedicated people of proven ability.

Invited to the French Lick meeting were such political, community and business leaders as Judge Charles W. Applegate, City Controller Fred L. Armstrong, State Senator Lawrence M. Borst, Gordon K. Durnil, Lucille Camp, Rexford C. Early, P.J. Finneran,

State Senator W. W. Hill, Jr., Mayor Richard G. Lugar, James T. Morris, John M. Mutz, Director of Public Works John W. Sweezy, and George B. Tintera. These individuals, under the leadership of Bulen, were to be the 1971 Lugar for Mayor Campaign Executive Committee.

The combined political experience of those assembled represented decades of success. Each was asked to summarize his or her views of the direction the campaign should pursue, his predictions for the issues to be faced, along with other essentials such as timing, advertising, problems to anticipate, and positive issues to stress. The meeting culminated with approximately forty committees being formed for the campaign. They were active and productive committees, with a great deal of authority. The membership of each committee was such that it intertwined with other committees to provide continuity of activity and purpose.

The policy decisions and coordination of the campaign was the responsibility of the Executive Committee, assembling every other week throughout the campaign. The official Lugar for Mayor Committee was formed and filed officially with County Clerk E. Allen Hunter, Harold Ransburg, and Kurt Pantzer, Sr. as co-chairmen. Mrs. Juan Solomon was named secretary and Pershing E. MacAllister took on responsibility as treasurer. The purpose of this official committee was to lend the experience and prestige of the officers, and their fund raising ability, to the campaign.

The Surveys and Public Opinion Committee was headed by a professional pollster. The Campaign Issue Committee, which would provide each candidate with a booklet of issues and answers, was headed by Attorney Robert N. Davies. Opposition Research was under the direction of Kurt F. Pantzer, Jr., who would delve into the public background of the Democrat candidates to determine their weaknesses and strengths. The Specific Research Committee, that was chaired by Carl R. Dortch, researched other cities of comparable size to make comparisons with Indianapolis. Gordon K. Durnil was named as campaign coordinator for the candidates, other than mayor, responsible for the coordination of the twenty five councilman district campaigns and conducting weekly seminars for the candidates to discuss issues and campaign strategy.

Candidate scheduling is always one of the key responsibilities of any campaign, and Mayor Lugar's schedule was to be jointly determined by Bulen and James T. Morris. Jean Jester also worked with Bulen and Morris on the mayor's schedule. Sarah Meeker coordinated the scheduling for the council candidates. Nick Longworth headed up the Advance and Security Committee, with the responsibility for determining in advance all details of where, and to whom, the mayor would be speaking. They examined the physical set up for all meetings and insured that each meeting would be executed as efficiently as possible. Nola Allen and Marilou Wertzler[1] had the responsibility of instructing the candidates' wives and families on their activities as an asset to the campaign.

As in 1967, only more extensively, John Sweezy was named chairman of the Special Mailing Committee. A large percentage of the success of the 1971 campaign depended upon Sweezy's committee. Computers were finding their way into campaigns and the purpose of Sweezy's committee was to send a personalized computer letter, that did not look like a computer letter, from Dick Lugar to every voter in the county. It was not to be a mass mailing, but instead a specialized endeavor with letters going to various special interest groups. Age, race, occupation, voting behavior, and localized problems, all were specialized categories in determining the subject matter of the mailings. The letters let voters know that the mayor had kept his word and that he knew what was going on in each voter's neighborhood. In essence, one paragraph of the mailings was worded similar to the following fictional example:

In 1967 I promised to put up a stop sign at 5th and Main. On June 1, 1968 the stop sign was installed. We also paved Main Street between 4th and 6th in your neighborhood during the summer of 1970, but I realize that you and your neighbors still have a drainage problem. If re-elected I will try to resolve it.

As chairman of the Data Processing Committee, George B. Tintera worked closely with Sweezy to determine the most workable and scientific methods of conducting the mailings.

A media committee was formed with the responsibility of all campaign advertising and news media coverage. Under the leadership of P. J. Finneran, the committee would coordinate the public relations of all candidates. A weekly newsletter committee was established with Robert D. Beckman, Jr. serving as editor. The newsletter was sent to everyone participating in the campaign. A Letter to the Editor Committee, with Marjorie O'Laughlin[2] as chairman, was formed to guarantee a fair shake in that section of the newspapers, and a speakers bureau was established to tell the Lugar story at community meetings. Deputy Mayor John W. Walls served as chairman of the speakers bureau.

Since Uni-Gov needed clarification, and because the voters are normally not willing to listen to, or read, long and detailed explanations, a Uni-Gov Digest was written. Nancy Foley was chairman of the committee to put together a booklet of one line explanations about unified government in Marion County. Larry S. Landis was named chairman of the committee which would outline the accomplishments of the Lugar Administration, and Jim Morris was the chairman of the Congratulations and Proclamations Committee. This latter committee would insure that any citizen who had achieved any degree of success would be recognized by the mayor. The birth of a baby, a 50th Wedding Anniversary, winning a high school athletic award, were all cause for recognition. As a result of this committee, which had operated throughout Mayor Lugar's term of office, there were few houses in Indianapolis that could not display a personalized letter from their mayor.

Organized under the regular Republican political party organization were various other committees. The candidate selection committee headed again by John Burkhart had the responsibility of recommending county-wide candidates. The preferred council candidates were selected by the precinct committeemen from the appropriate districts. The coordination of the overall campaign with the Republican campaigns in the other cities and towns was the responsibility of Judge Charlie Applegate, and the many Republican clubs in the county were coordinated by Fred Monschien. Each of the nine townships opened campaign headquarters.

Fred Armstrong led the registration and absent voters drive, with Robert W. Messick concentrating on apartment complexes. Armstrong also was responsible for election day supplies, with the election day slates being the responsibility of Rex Early. Lawrence L. Buell was chairman of the Voter Turnout Committee; Lucille Camp was responsible for the campaign involvement of patronage personnel, and attorney Charles G. Castor was chairman of the Security and Legal Committee.

Sherry B. Gardiner, wife of a prominent Indianapolis physician Sprague H. Gardiner, coordinated the council candidate selection in the 25 council districts. Sherry was another phenomena of the Bulen era. She had volunteered to work a few days a week in the 1966 campaign and soon thereafter became indispensable. Throughout the entire tenure of Bulen's chairmanship, Sherry worked day and night, seven days a week, for no pay, and she continued her role under Chairman Sweezy as Secretary of the Marion County Republican Central Committee.

Another key factor in any campaign is citizen involvement. If a voter has a job in the campaign, or if the voter contributes at some level, in money, time or ability, he or she will surely vote for your candidates. The volunteer is also likely to convince family and friends to vote the same way. It is often easy to enlist new faces to a campaign, especially with a good candidate. The hard part is to keep those people interested and on the team. If a person is asked to be on a committee, and the committee has no real function, that person may become irritated and desert the cause. To bring in new people, to use volunteers effectively, and to keep them involved in Republican political activity, Bulen asked John M. Mutz to chair the Volunteers for Lugar Committee. Mutz, a highly talented businessman and well liked Republican, immediately began to organize. A Lugar volunteer headquarters was opened with Dell Chumley as headquarters manager. The Lugar headquarters was not to be the normal political office located in an old and dilapidated building. It was, instead, on the ground floor of a modern building, located away from the downtown area. Plentiful lighted parking was available, and the decor of the headquarters was clean, bright, and well done with donated furniture and carpeting. It was a headquarters for volunteers, not for the normal political types—a headquarters where housewives could come without fear and without worrying about soiling their clothing.

Various Lugar committees were organized by Mutz: committees for doctors, clergy, lawyers, dentists, engineers, teachers, veterans, blacks, ethnics, religious groups, labor, youth, senior citizens, democrats, independents, and others. All of the committees advocated the re-election of Dick Lugar, and all were real people, planning real projects to assist in that endeavor. There were no "paper committees" in Bulen's well planned campaign to re-elect Dick Lugar as Mayor of Indianapolis. One of those new committees was the Indianapolis WINs—Women In Neighborhood Service—led by Scotty Bennent. Their mission was to be the heart of the Republican Party, to concentrate on the needs of the unfortunate in the community, and specifically, to concentrate on the narcotics problem in their city. This new concept not only would educate the many Republican women involved, but it would give them a humanitarian purpose under the umbrella of the Republican Party. On a citizen to citizen level, WINs addressed the basic needs of the community.

This may seem a long dissertation on the many players involved in the 1971 Lugar for Mayor campaign organization, but the truth is that only a few of the individuals involved have been named. The organizational manual listing all those involved could be a book in itself. The complexity and the workability of the 1971 campaign is an attestation of Keith Bulen's organizational ability. As only the second month of the campaign rolled around, the organization was functioning smoothly. The committees were meeting regularly and, most importantly, they were meeting the deadlines set by Bulen. The plans were drafted. The headquarters was ready and open. And, at this point, all Dick Lugar needed was a Democratic opponent.

---

1. Marilou Wertzler was the elected Reporter of the Indiana State Courts.
2. Marge O'Laughlin was elected City Clerk along with Mayor Lugar in 1967. She later was elected as Clerk of the State Courts and as Treasurer of the state of Indiana.

Chapter Ten

As the May, 1971 primary election approached, it became obvious to the Republican leadership who Lugar's opponent would be. Although the local Democrat Organization was factionalized, and as many as seven hopefuls declared their intent to seek the Democrat nomination for mayor, John F. Neff, a bright, young attorney, was the front-runner and on May 4th he was nominated. Lugar also had opposition in the primary. However, few doubted that he would be easily nominated, causing the Bulen team to worry about apathy within the organization. Bulen wanted a good showing in the primary, to propel the mayor into the fall campaign.

To combat apathy Bulen attempted another first. He called an off-year county convention where the mayor and county chairman, at their eloquent best, attempted to build a fire under the assembled precinct workers. The Mayor's 100 Percent Club was announced at the convention. Any precinct committeemen who could equal or better his precinct vote of the 1970 Primary Election, would be named a member of the Mayor's 100 Percent Club. Over 150 committeemen and ward chairman passed the 100 percent mark, some even exceeded 150 percent, and Mayor Lugar was easily renominated. Lugar received 35,878 votes in the Republican primary, over 12,000 more votes than his Democrat opponent received from his party. In fact, Mayor Lugar received more votes than did all seven candidates for mayor in the Democrat primary election.

As the primary election passed, the 1971 campaign began in earnest. Dick Lugar, the only Republican mayor of a major city in the United States, took on John Neff, a former State Representative, who had acquitted himself well in Democratic circles.

As the campaign was launched with the opening of the Volunteers for Lugar Headquarters, local Republicans were jubilant in the belief that Lugar was a sure winner. The campaign leadership viewed the situation differently. It was true that Lugar had high name recognition, that his administration had a good record, and that Lugar had, in fact, put Indianapolis on the national map, but there was always that other truth to consider. There were more Democrats in Marion County than there were Republicans. The same old formula held true. To win Lugar had to receive 90 percent of the Republican vote, 65 percent of the Independent vote, and 15 percent of the Democratic vote. If the Democrats could turn out their vote, they would win, irrespective of what the Republicans could do.

To turn out the Democrat vote, John Neff brought in the highly expensive Matthew Reese Agency. Reese had accomplished fantastic results for President John F. Kennedy in 1960 and for President Lyndon Johnson in 1964. He had also been in Indiana before. In 1968 he moved Robert F. Kennedy to an unexpected primary victory, and in the fall he helped re-elect Senator Birch Bayh (D-IN) while President Nixon and the rest of the Republican state ticket were winning by huge pluralities. In 1970, hired by Democrat Senator Vance Hartke, Reese worked in three counties, accounting for approximately 10,000 additional votes in Allen county, another 10,000 in St. Joseph County, and approximately 5,000 in Marion County. The official tabulation listed Hartke the winner by less than 4,000 votes, and Matt Reese could claim at least 25,000 votes that he had garnered for Hartke.

Bulen and the Lugar campaign leadership knew of Reese's talents and respected his abilities. The 1971 campaign for mayor of Indianapolis was not so much a Lugar versus Neff battle. Had such been the case, Lugar could have won hands down. Instead it became a battle between the best organizational politician the national Democratic Party could put on the field—Matt Reese—and the Marion County Republican Party, probably the best political organization in the nation.

It was Bulen's job to eliminate what apathy might exist in his organization, and to do with volunteers what Reese would do with his highly financed professional operation. The secret to Republican success was to turn out the Republican votes in the suburbs to counteract Reese's activity with inner city residents, and traditional Democrat block voters.

The battle shaping up was the kind best understood by Indiana politicians, not so much candidate versus candidate, as in other states, but organization versus organization. Each of the more than 600 precinct committeemen in Marion County were called upon to canvass the voters in their precincts. To know who was Republican, Democrat, or Independent. To know who was for or against Lugar. To know who needed to be registered to vote, who needed absentee ballots, who needed rides to the polls or any other form of voter assistance. The deadline for completing the precinct polls was September 1st. It had to be done by then to give campaign management sufficient time to assess and act upon the information.

Bulen saw the need to firm up Republican voters. He wanted more than the necessary ninety percent. He printed a booklet explaining in simple terms how unified government was working in Marion County. Much of the misinformation about Uni-Gov was rampant in the high Republican suburban areas of the county.

Campaign Communicators, Inc. was formed in 1971 to produce advertising and conduct public relations for the full campaign effort. Keith Bulen served as Chairman of the Board of Directors and Gordon K. Durnil served as President. Both of them had achieved a degree of expertise in the area of campaign management. Mitchell E. Daniels, Jr.[1] was Vice President. Daniels and Patrick J. Finneran supervised a staff of political public relations and advertising specialists.

Each of the various campaign committees met throughout the summer months, and by summer's end they had completed most of their assignments. Campaign Communicators, Inc. was producing two thirty minute television documentaries—one about Lugar the man, and the other about the accomplishments of his administration. Also in the hopper were radio and television spot commercials, newspaper advertisements, and a full color brochure. Each of the council candidates were calling upon voters, wherever they could be found, to sell themselves and the Lugar team. Each of the 34 candidates had a personalized brochure that also listed every candidate on the Republican ticket.

One campaign "shocker" came at 8:05 PM on June 30th. It was at that time that Ohio became the 38th state to ratify the 26th Amendment to the United States Constitution. From that point on, 18, 19, and 20 year olds, were allowed to vote. Dick Lugar had long advocated the eighteen-year-old vote, but no one really knew what the political impact would be. Lugar and Bulen wanted the new voters in the G.O.P. camp. Two youth organizations under the Volunteer For Lugar Committee were already in operation, "New Voters For Lugar" and "New Voices For Lugar." These two committees immediately began registering the new voters, and soliciting them to the Lugar cause.

Another "shocker" came in August, when a Federal Court decision on racial balance in the Indianapolis schools was rendered. The dictum of the decision implied that Uni-Gov might require the abolition of local and separate school systems within the county. The truth was that the Uni-Gov law protected and kept separate the eleven school districts of Marion County. Armed with the dictum, John Neff inserted the first false issue of the campaign with the hopes of playing upon the emotional opposition to busing school children for racial balance. It was a false issue because in Marion County civil government had no voice in school affairs, and because Mayor Lugar was on record as being opposed to busing for racial balance.

As Labor Day approached, the traditional kick-off date for campaigns, the campaign for mayor of Indianapolis was well under way. John Neff was riding city buses in the hopes of building name recognition, while Dick Lugar was speaking to and visiting four to five groups a day as he also continued to run the city government. In the trenches doing the work that would decide the election outcome were Matt Reese and the Marion County Republican Organization.

That first municipal election under unified government in Indianapolis is worth historic notice. It was another first for a vibrant city that was celebrating its sesquicentennial in 1971. Where there had previously been a city council and a separate county council, there was now to be one unified council to serve as the legislative body for the entire county which now became Indianapolis. The old system provided for at-large election of council members, but under Uni-Gov the council was broken into twenty five districts, moving representation in city government a step closer to the citizenry. The twenty five Republican district candidates in the first Uni-Gov election were

Gordon G. Gilmer, Beurt R. SerVaas, William G. Schneider, William A. Dowden, Harold J. Egenes, Stephen R. West, Thomas C. Hasbrook, Jack F. Patterson, Lillian M. Davis, Robbie Beckweth, Avis C. Bell, Donald R. McPherson and Richard F. Clark. Also running in that first election were Beverley K. Miller, A. Clark Elmore, Mark Bell, Gerry M. Finch, Dwight L. Cottingham, Kenneth N. Giffin, Joe T. Gorham, Thomas A. Caito, Lester R. Neal, Alan L. Crapo, Donald N. Griffith and William K. Byrum. Also to be elected were four at-large councilmen representing the entire county. Those candidates were Roger W. Brown, Alan R. Kimbell, William A. Leak and John C. Ruckelshaus. The two new criminal court judge candidates were Republicans Harold H. Kohlmeyer, Jr., and John B. Wilson, Jr.

Two other events occurred in 1971 that old time politicos agreed were "firsts" in Marion County. One of the State Representatives elected in 1970, Choice Edwards, resigned to take a position with the Federal Government, and State Senator W. W. Hill, Jr., also elected in 1970, resigned to assume the chairmanship of the Indiana Public Service Commission. As the result of these two resignations two special election orders were drafted and signed by Governor Whitcomb calling for a special election for these two offices to also be combined with the 1971 municipal elections. The novelty of these two special elections was twofold. First, 1971 was the beginning year for annual sessions for the State Legislature, and 1971 was also the first municipal election in which all voters in Marion County could participate. Without those two circumstances, it would not have been possible to hold the special elections for criminal court and state legislative openings. John M. Mutz was selected to fill the vacant State Senator candidacy and Reverend Lawrence R. Voelker filled the State Representative spot, becoming the first Catholic priest to serve in the Indiana General Assembly.

So, as the management and workers of both parties were doing grass roots work on the mechanics of politics, the 34 Republican candidates were covering the county, meeting people, and soliciting votes.

The issue of forced busing of school children for racial balance ultimately raised its ugly head as the prime issue of the campaign. The Democrat candidate tried to assume a posture of opposing busing, implying all the while that Lugar favored the decision to bus children to schools throughout the county. Actually, the Federal Court decision made clear that the Uni-Gov law held separate the local systems and, if anything, it prevented busing. Bulen decided that the Lugar position on busing should be made abundantly clear, so he purchased a thirty-minute segment on local television for the mayor to state the facts. The speech, which had the benefit of close political scrutiny, was not orated in the normal Lugar prose, but in a style of simplicity so that all could measure the truth of the matter and dismiss the false issue of busing from the municipal campaign.

The bright side of Lugar advertising was the two half-hour documentaries that played two to five times a day during the last weeks of the campaign. The documentaries were professionally done by Campaign Communicators, Inc. They stimulated pride in Indianapolis, an All-American City, extolled the virtues of Indianapolis and the progress made under Lugar, and reminded voters of the Lugar character, talent, and his dedication to their needs.

The myriad of plans laid down in December and January by Bulen and his political brain trust were successfully executed with finesse in September and October. Everything worked. The best Republican metropolitan organization in the nation was up for the battle and won on all fronts, with strong support from first-time voters, and heavy support from labor, minorities, Jewish, and other traditional non-Republican voters.

Another major key to Lugar's 1971 success was a voter turnout program, conceived by Bulen, that probably surpassed any ever attempted in a metropolitan area up until that time. The name of each and every registered voter in the county was placed on computer tape, with information obtained by precinct committeemen from door-to-door polling, and personalized letters from the mayor were received by every registered voter who was not a dyed-in-the-wool Democrat. All specialized lists of organizations were copied and each member received a personalized letter from Lugar. In every case the letter was personalized and localized to discuss areas and/or issues in which the voter receiving the letter was interested. And finally, on the day preceding the election, every household that was not inhabited by Democrats, received a telegram asking them to vote for Mayor Lugar, telling them where their polling place was located, the hours that the polls would be open, and the importance of their vote. George Tintera, who headed up the voter turnout project, didn't get much sleep during August, September, and October.

As a back-up to the letter writing campaign, a strong and efficient telephone operation was put into effect as one more aspect of voter turnout. Neighborhood blitzes of young people knocking on doors promoting the Lugar cause gave more emphasis to the bandwagon that was rolling toward a Lugar landslide. All of this was in addition to the normal duties of highly dedicated precinct committeemen who conducted their regularly efficient get-out-the-votes efforts in their own precincts. The get-out-the-vote effort worked to such a degree, that a phone call was received at Lugar Headquarters on election day from an elderly lady stating that she did not intend to vote. She complained that she had received several telephone calls urging her to vote for Lugar, and that three young people had already been to her door, the last of whom let her cat out. Approximately one half hour later the same woman called back saying that she would now vote for Lugar, because a fourth young man had come to her door, had retrieved the cat, and was waiting to escort her to the polls.

As evening fell on election day 1971 in Indianapolis, the highly reputed Matt Reese was sent scampering as Lugar registered a massive victory. The victory set these records:

1. The voter turnout was the highest ever for a municipal election in Indiana.

2. Lugar's plurality and total vote shattered all previous records as he received over 60 percent of the vote.

3. Lugar became the first Indianapolis mayor since 1900 to win re-election—the first Republican to ever accomplish that feat.

4. For the first time in the Twentieth Century, a political organization of either party won a fifth consecutive countywide victory in Marion County.

The win marked Chairman Bulen's 17th consecutive electoral success, including conventions, primaries, and general elections, and Bulen savored that 17th win probably more than any other. He had at last executed the perfect campaign, against the toughest Democrat political professionals of the time.

---

1. Mitch Daniels later served in many high level positions, including Administrative Assistant to Senator Lugar and White House Political Advisor to President Reagan.

Chapter Eleven

Nineteen seventy-two was to be Bulen's greatest year, but as it dawned, he had many thoughts on his mind. When he assumed the chairmanship of the Marion County Republican Central Committee, he stated that he would step down gracefully and not attempt to hold on until the last straw, as so many political leaders are wont to do. In 1972, therefore, he did step down and handed the reins of the county organization over to the able leadership of John Sweezy.

Bulen moved his office into the facilities of Campaign Communicators, Inc., where he could direct the activities of again carrying Indiana for President Nixon, direct several other campaigns, and perform his duties as Republican Chairman of the 11th Congressional District of Indiana, and as Republican National Committeeman from Indiana (a post to which he was re-elected for a second four-year term in June, 1972). Campaign Communicators, Inc. also served under Bulen's direction as the promotional agency for Mayor Richard G. Lugar on a national scale. On the staff at Campaign Communicators, other than Durnil and Daniels, were Ruby Miller, Secretary-Treasurer, and Terry Gardiner. There was also one full-time volunteer whose loyalty and service to Keith Bulen extended over decades. A precinct committeeman and active in many community affairs, Mrs Dwight Schuster handled special projects for Bulen on a near full time, non-paid, basis. A little later, the effervescent Dottie Daniels, mother of Mitch, joined as a regular volunteer.

By 1972 Bulen had been instrumental in electing Presidents, governors, mayors, and various other state and local officials, but one challenge had eluded him. In 1964 during the Goldwater loss, the 11th Congressional District of Indiana (Indianapolis) had been won by Andrew Jacobs (D-Ind). In 1965, a Democrat controlled state legislature had drawn the lines to make the 11th a safe district for the Democrats. The lines were redrawn in 1967, but it still remained safe for Andy Jacobs. Finally in 1971, the lines were drawn to give Republicans a fighting chance for victory.

A hard-fought primary fight ensued between William Hudnut, a Presbyterian minister, and Danny Burton, the 1970 GOP nominee. Following a voluntary recount of the votes, Bill Hudnut was declared the winner by 98 votes. Bulen, as 11th District Chairman, made that contest, Bill Hudnut versus Andy Jacobs, his number one project for the fall.

Another important duty fell upon Bulen's broad political shoulders in 1972. The Republican Party in Indiana was in a bad state of disharmony, and early polls indicated that a Republican candidate for governor would have little chance of success against former Democrat governor, Matthew Welsh. President Nixon's chances of carrying Indiana were also in jeopardy due to the political infighting. Bulen gave the state organizational problems his concentration, and he was one hundred percent successful in bringing harmony back into the party. He was instrumental in having James T. Neal, a true peace maker and decisive leader, elected as Chairman of the Indiana Republican State Central Committee. After some battles for the gubernatorial nomination in the state convention, Bulen worked with state leaders to bring the entire Republican leadership into the camp of Otis R. Bowen, immediately after Bowen's nomination.

At the 1972 Republican National Convention in Miami, Bulen had another plan—to make sure that every delegate knew about Dick Lugar. A newspaper was printed in Indianapolis and flown to Miami in the middle of the night for deposit at each delegate's hotel room door. The newspaper highlighted the successes of Mayor Lugar in Indianapolis. Bulen also organized a reception at The Fontainebleu Hotel to which he invited every delegate from across the nation. and most showed up to shake hands with Lugar and eat highly expensive gourmet foods. Warren Spangle made sure the event was well done, even enlisting volunteers to count dirty plates so Bulen wouldn't be overcharged. Bulen also arranged for private dinners with the "stars" of the national media, so they too could get to know the qualities of Dick Lugar.

Bulen was also responsible for combining the Indiana Nixon campaign, and the campaign for governor and state offices, into one coordinated effort. Will H. Hays, Jr., the Chairman of The Indiana Committee for The Re-election of the President, John B. King, campaign manager for Otis Bowen, Chairman Neal, Keith Bulen, Gordon Durnil, Clarence Long, Robert Morris, and others worked in complete concert throughout the year, seeking a Republican sweep in Indiana.

Specific Bulen projects in the 1972 statewide election, on behalf of the President, Governor Otis Bowen, and all candidates, included an elaborate direct mail campaign. Personalized letters were sent to Republican and Independent voters a week before the election. The letters not only contained the name of the voter in the body of the letter, they were localized to the city or county of the recipient. Telegrams were also sent to Republican and Independent voters urging them to vote for Otis Bowen and the Republican candidate for Congress in their area. It also told them where to vote and the hours that the polls were open. The letter was in message form on White House stationery over the name of President Richard M. Nixon who was extremely popular among Hoosier voters. These mailings were once again the result of many volunteers accumulating the names of registered voters in Indiana, and having these names computerized. The result was that 691,000 households of potential favorable voters were contacted.

The accumulation of the targeted voter lists were supervised by Lois Earle of the Indiana Committee for the Re-election of the President. George Tintera was again responsible for all mechanical details of the computerization, as well as the printing and mailing of well over one million pieces of mail. A statewide telephone campaign was also conducted from the computer sheets under the supervision of Marilou Wertzler. The fourth use of the computerized registered voters list was a door to door get-out-the-vote blitz under the direction of Edwin J. Simcox.[1]

A statewide magazine newspaper insert, another Bulen idea, was again used in statewide newspapers. Bulen was also responsible for labor union endorsements and support in both the Nixon and Bowen campaigns, and he brought many national dignitaries into the state to campaign for Republican candidates.

The result of Bulen's leadership was a landslide for the Republican Party in Indiana on November 7, 1972. President Nixon received a record plurality of 700,000 votes. Governor Bowen won by a record 300,000 votes, all Republican state candidates were successful by landslide margins, and for the first time in eight years, the 11th Congressional District of Indiana was represented by a Republican, Congressman William H. Hudnut. Two other Republican Congressmen, William G. Bray (6th District) and Elwood (Bud) Hillis (5th District), who also represented portions of Indianapolis, were easily re-elected with Bulen assistance.

A more specific reference to the expertise and effectiveness of Keith Bulen and his successor John Sweezy was the 104,000 plurality for President Nixon, and the 41,000 plurality for Governor Bowen that were obtained in Marion County. With landslide victories for national, state, and local candidates, and the election of Bill Hudnut, Bulen admitted that 1972 was his greatest year as a political pro.

---

1. Ed Simcox later served as Indiana Secretary of State.

Chapter Twelve

As the author brings his writings to a conclusion in late 1972, having examined briefly a six year period of dynamic leadership by a man who has cared enough about his fellow citizens to devote his professional life to a necessary cause that others may demean and shirk, and to sacrifice his personal life for the same cause, it is difficult for the author to write "The End" to such a story.

Knowing Keith Bulen, his plans, his talents, his desires, and his concerns, the author ends this discourse in 1972 with a belief that this surely is only the beginning.

Chapter Thirteen
Addendum 1974

Nineteen seventy-three was a year of anticipation and preparation for the important 1974 U.S. Senate race in Indiana. Democrat Birch Bayh had won election in 1962 over incumbent Homer Capehart, re-election in 1968 over challenger Bill Ruckelshaus, and he was likely to seek his third term as a United States Senator in 1974, but in 1973 Bulen was grooming his strongest candidate. Mayor Richard G. Lugar traveled throughout the nation, into over one half of the states, to speak and attract the attention of Republican leaders. Lugar was becoming a national figure, and his name started appearing on public opinion surveys as someone with Presidential potential. Bulen also traveled the nation as he tested the waters and touted Lugar to his colleagues on the Republican National Committee. He also boasted about the strong political organization supporting Dick Lugar.

As 1973 moved on, Watergate and its attendant tragedies crowded other news into oblivion, and doubt rose as to the wisdom of a Lugar candidacy in 1974. The same dilemma faced Republican leaders in other states. Should they run their best candidate or a sacrificial lamb to absorb the disdain of the voters? Bulen had never defaulted an election and he wasn't about to start in 1974. He spent much of 1973 meeting with Republican county leaders all throughout Indiana and he put together a coalition to guarantee Mayor Dick Lugar the Republican nomination for the U.S. Senate. Bulen, Durnil, and Daniels attended the first Republican National Committee Campaign Manager College in Los Angeles in December of 1973. The week in California was instructional, but Bulen and his two aides spent most of the time laying out a campaign plan for the 1974 Lugar campaign.

The 1974 Republican U.S. Senate campaign was the best planned, best executed, and best financed statewide campaign in Hoosier history. From the very technical computerized direct mail mail program, to the door-to-door volunteer blitz, all programs worked as expected. The statewide volunteer telephone campaign became a model for other states to emulate. There was also party harmony, not common in Republican circles at the time. Governor Otis Bowen, Lieutenant Governor Bob Orr, State Chairman Thomas Milligan, and a strong consensus of the Republican leadership worked together toward a common goal.

Everything was with Bulen in his attempt to elect a Republican Senator except the voters. All year long the professional surveys indicated some problems, but Lugar was close to incumbent Birch Bayh in the head-to-head race and each day he was moving closer. But it was a year when voters were turned off by events in Washington, when Republicans were reluctant to admit that they were Republicans. It was a year of resignation from the oval office. It was a year of trials of public officials, a year when new President Gerald Ford pardoned the former President Dick Nixon, who was responsible for Ford being President. The people were angry. It was also a year of high prices and unemployment fears, and it became a year when when Republican voters pulled the Democrat lever in the voting booths throughout America. It was a year for Republicans to lose, and lose they did.

Long before the election was held, Keith Bulen announced that he was retiring from politics and that he would resign from his party posts at the end of 1974. Bulen had sacrificed his adult life for the good of his city, state, nation, and party. He deserved a rest. His dedication to good government led him to pursue quality candidates for public office, help them in their elections, and then sit back with pride as those people served the public trust with integrity. He captained the ship of organizational politics as a master practitioner, knowing always that the strength of party politics was at the precinct level. He fought to preserve the two-party system, and, as a result, Indiana in 1974 was a bastion of political party viability.

At a time in the American experience when many in the news media were intent upon destroying those who would promote the value of a two-party political system, and a time when those engaged in democratic debate and in the free and competitive electoral system were being chastised in the birthing of political correctness, and at a time immediately after the Watergate scandal when the public was becoming fed up with politicians, and a time when television consultants where filling the vacuums left by the fading political parties, Keith Bulen stood tall. He conducted his adversarial political combat with civility. He respected his opponents, and that was especially true of the person leading the Democratic charge, State Chairman Gordon St. Angelo—a tenacious foe, but a genteel man. But most of all, Keith loved America and he respected the system where volunteerism, not governmental dictates, kept the gears of the free electoral process turning

Would Keith Bulen really retire from politics?

Could he?

Chapter Fourteen
Author Observations

The preceding account is from long ago, though it doesn't seem so long since I was living and learning in those exciting times. My grandchildren are now older than were my children back during the Bulen Era. They were times of turmoil—racial unrest, war, urban disorder, youthful rebellion, and assassination. They were also times where proof is abundant that one person, dedicated to a proposition, with loyal friends, can change the world. I know the truth of that claim. I've seen it happen, I've been a part of it, but it's a hard proposition to sell to young Americans as the twentieth century comes to a close. American "can-do-ism" has somehow dithered to "let someone else do it." Even worse, too many people don't care about our civic well-being. They claim that government is not relevant to their lives. In the 1996 Presidential election, across this great "land of the free and home of the brave," 51% of the voters who bothered to get registered to vote, *did not* show up at the polls. It's hard not to wonder—can we sustain a democratic republic if over one-half of American voters don't bother to vote?

These were not questions for Keith, because his view was that we can do today what we have previously done, if we give it an outstanding effort. Keith believed in volunteerism. Keith believed that political leaders should be visionary, strong, but accountable. He was proud of his nation and those who sacrificed so much for our freedoms. He believed that a good understanding of our history could help us find the right path for the future. He believed in tradition. He believed in loyalty. He believed that the American spirit is alive, if not well, and that it is our responsibility to rekindle it. Such is the challenge for the annual Bulen Symposium on American Politics in Indianapolis, Indiana.

As I wrote the 1974 addendum, I gingerly touched on some distasteful times when I mentioned those who would destroy lives. It was a bigger problem than that, and it was still worrisome as I was writing back then. After the fall of Nixon, and after Gerald Ford assumed the presidency, various law enforcement agencies of the federal government joined together as a task force to "chase" a few Nixon supporters from around the nation. In Indiana, the target was Keith Bulen. The Internal Revenue Service led the charge and went after friends of Bulen with threats of prosecution if they didn't "rat" on Keith, and there were no friendly "spin doctors" around in those days to support Keith and his friends. The papers ran daily negative stories about Keith, and for years thereafter, whenever his name was mentioned in the paper, the negative words reappeared as if by magic. The reporters "mysteriously" knew when and where the federal agents would track down another friend of Bulen for all of the neighbors to observe. Several local lawyers billed big fees, others volunteered their time and expertise, and finally, after four years, Keith and his friends were exonerated of any wrongdoing. The government dropped the whole stupid thing by sending out form letters to those who had been threatened by their own government—a government they had helped to mold.

Keith Bulen accomplished great things. He was always a stickler for following even the most vague aspects of election law. He didn't deserve to have his reputation tarnished by reporters and especially by agents of the federal government. It was all a lot of nonsense, but it created a conundrum for me as I watched the 1998 "White House In Crisis" on television as the special prosecutor investigated President Clinton. My partisan instincts caused me to feel allegiance to those chasing the President, but the familiar tactics of federal law enforcement agents caused a churning in the pit of my gut—a grim remembrance of 1974 governmental wrongs.

Keith did not retire in 1974. He went on with the practice of law and with his interest in Standardbred horse racing and breeding. It became his avocation. He owned world champion Abercrombie, voted Harness Horse of the Year in 1978, and he served as a Director and President of the Indiana Standardbred Association. He was inducted into the Indiana Standardbred Hall of Fame in 1997.

What about politics after 1974? A detailed resume appears in the final pages, but here's a taste of Keith's political actively after his 1974 "retirement." He was the Honorary Chairman of the 1984 Indiana Republican State Convention, and he was a delegate to the Republican National Conventions of 1976, 1980, and 1984. He was responsible for successful Indiana primary election campaigns for Ronald Reagan in 1976 and 1980. He was Reagan's national convention coordinator in 1976, Deputy Chairman of the National Reagan for President Committee in 1980, and the Eastern Coordinator (17 states) for Reagan-Bush. He then was Associate Director of Presidential Personnel during the transition period after Reagan was elected.

In 1981, President Reagan appointed Keith to be United States Commissioner on the International Joint Commission, United States and Canada, and he was confirmed by the United States Senate. His task on the commission was to resolve and prevent problems between the United States and Canada, mostly environmental problems. David LaRoche, in his essay, has more to say about Keith's prowess on the international scene. In 1988, Keith was a Senior Advisor for the Bush for President campaign, he worked in various Hoosier statewide campaigns, he headed up Victory '90 Indiana House and Senate campaigns, and he was elected to the Indiana House of Representatives in 1990.

He couldn't quit because he cared too much!

Throughout 1998, Keith offered advice to numerous state and federal campaigns even though the agony of cancer was corroding his body. Externally, he was pretty much the same old Keith, other than for the loss of hair from toxic medication. The battle against cancer differed from other battles he had waged and won. His mind still sharp. His loyal volunteers were ready to for war. But no plan could be conceived, other than to trust in God.

With his daughters at his side, Keith Bulen passed away in the early morning hours of January 4, 1999.

WHAT OTHERS SAY ABOUT KEITH BULEN:

Throwing Chairs and Raising Hell

by Jack Colwell

L. Keith Bulen, proud to be known as a professional politician, and rightly so, never set out to win popularity contests. So, he didn't. He set out to win elections. That he did. There is much of which Keith Bulen can be proud. Most significant is the way he used his base of power as Marion County Republican chairman to launch the political career of a school board member who has become one of the most respected members of the United States Senate, indeed, respected internationally. The launching of that career—of Senator Richard G. Lugar—was one of those times when Keith didn't win popularity even among his own ward chairmen in Indianapolis.

"They started throwing chairs and raising hell," Keith once told me of the reaction at a meeting during which he announced his support of the relatively unknown Lugar as the Republican challenger in 1967 to an incumbent Democratic mayor entrenched in city hall.

"I told my people we had to pick the highest type candidate if we were going to win, and he (Lugar) was my choice," Keith related.

His choice prevailed, for the nomination and in the fall election. Lugar won a mayor's office long in Democratic hands. He also was to win acclaim for changing the image of Indianapolis, from sleepy to thriving. Implementation of "Unigov," with guidance from Keith, was a key factor in both the revitalization of Indianapolis and establishing a national reputation for Lugar. Also, no Democrat has since been elected mayor of Indianapolis.

Some Democrats believe the combined city-county government was just a plot by Keith to ensure Republican mayors. As a smart politician, he certainly realized the possibility of that. But the combination has proved to be good government. And it illustrates the classic Bulen contention that good government is good politics and the best way to win elections is to seek out the best and brightest of candidates who will govern well.

Keith told me that he realized he sometimes brought problems for himself, even as he brought victories for his candidates, by his bluntness and playing-to-win elections, not friends. The dark days when he was savaged in *Indianapolis Star* newspaper articles that made him a target of a federal strike-force investigation (which eventually found no basis for charges) were in part, in Keith's view, the result of his declining to bring candidates to the newspaper's publisher for an official blessing, as prior Republican leaders in Indianapolis had traditionally done.

The political expertise of Keith Bulen extended to the national level. He was deputy chairman for Ronald Reagan's 1980 campaign for the Republican presidential nomination. Again, Keith's all-out effort to win one for the Gipper brought some enemies right in the Reagan camp. At Reagan's 1980 election-night victory celebration, campaign advance men held up a sign, captured in a photo in *The New York Times*, expressing their view of Bulen: "Will Rogers Never Met Keith Bulen." Keith shrugged it off with this explanation: "Advance men think they ought to drive big cars, stay in the presidential suite and impress girls in the cities they work, then charge it all to the campaign committee." Instead, Keith insisted on emphasizing the work of advance work and keeping within the campaign budget.

While many Bulen proteges in addition to Lugar have gone on to distinguished careers and to express admiration for their mentor, Keith didn't hesitate to tell some of them as he ran their campaigns to refrain from trying to be their own campaign managers. Keith once observed that candidates, so personally involved, are the least objective in making campaign strategy decisions. Also, they must win friends, avoid making enemies. That's one of the reasons why a campaign pro such as Keith is needed to make decisions that are necessary to win, necessary sometimes if a good candidate is going to go on to seek good government, but not necessarily likely to win friends for the decision maker.

Keith Bulen made those necessary decisions, winning elections and, yes, even making friends among those in both parties who admire a real professional doing his best to seek the best that his party can offer in elections and in office.

Jack Colwell is the veteran political writer for The South Bend Tribune.

What is a Politician?

Pundits tend to refer to anyone who is in any way connected to government or political activity as a politician. Professional politicians don't see it that way. As you can see from the following remarks, Lyn Nofziger, a consummate "working politician," separates out candidates from that denotation. Most professionals see the mass that are labeled as politicians in three groups. The many are "governmental workers." The most noticed are "candidates and office holders." But the ones who make it all happen are the people in the trenches, who promote, plan, and execute. They are the ones entitled to wear the title of "politician." They are not looking for cushy government jobs, nor do their egos demand that reporters write and talk about them. They don't get much credit for winning, but they often get the blame for losing. Those of us who are proud to think of ourselves as "politicians" are reluctant to share the title. Even so, we would declare Keith Bulen, and the writer of the next essay, as "politicians extraordinaire."

The Three Best

by Lyn Nofziger

If I had to pick the three best working politicians (as opposed to candidates) in my time in politics they would be, in no particular order, F. Clifton White, Stuart Spencer, and Keith Bulen.

The common denominator among them would be their superb political instincts. All three could run a campaign for you better than anyone I know. Clif White and Keith Bulen were also tremendous organizers and either or both could put together a national convention organization as well or better than those who have come after them or went before.

Bulen and White should have been Republican National Chairmen. I don't think Spencer would have taken the job if it had been offered to him. White missed his chance when Barry Goldwater, who didn't quite trust White because he was an easterner, failed to name him chairman following the 1964 Republican National Convention.

Bulen was never enough of a "nice guy" to be elected by the national committee or selected by a presidential nominee. His problem: He didn't suffer fools gladly. In fact, he hardly suffered them at all. But at the same time he was admired greatly by his fellows in the ranks of the party's professional politicians, men and women who know the importance of organization.

Over the years Keith also taught and developed a cadre of competent younger operatives who are still making their mark in the party.

It was my good fortune to know and work with—and learn from—all three men over the last 35 years. All three, at one time or another in their careers, were involved with Ronald Reagan's campaigns either for governor or president and all three can claim some credit for Reagan's political successes. Keith ran Reagan's operation at the 1980 Republican National Convention in Detroit and I have not seen a better, smoother, operation. He also ran some Reagan regional operations in both 1976 and 1980.

The Republican Party could use operatives like any of this trio today, but I suspect it will be a long time before we see their likes again.

Lyn Nofziger describes himself as an early Reganite who was involved with Reagan from his first campaign for governor through his last campaign for President. Other professional campaign managers would describe Lyn as one of the 20th Century's best politicians.

Master Statesman

by Earl L. Butz

A master statesman has been defined as one who can coalesce divergent groups behind a single banner to achieve a political or legislative objective. Keith Bulen proved himself to be such a statesman at each of the various political and governmental posts in which he served.

He was an effective political leader because the public credit for his victories usually rested on shoulders other than his own. It has been said that a great leader can accomplish the impossible, so long as the leader doesn't care who gets credit for the successful deed.

Keith was such a leader in the latter half of the 20th century. How do I know? I was a "victim" of his political leadership at the 1968 Indiana Republican State Convention in Indianapolis. At that time, the major political parties nominated candidates for the top statewide offices in convention, rather than in primary elections. I was one of three candidates for governor. The other two candidates were Dr. Otis Bowen from Plymouth and Ed Whitcomb from Seymour. Ed's campaign was managed by Keith Bulen.

In any contest with three candidates, it is possible for the winner to emerge with less than a majority vote. All that is needed is a plurality, followed by the withdrawal of the candidate with the least support. On that first ballot in 1968, I was the "low man on the totem pole." On the next ballot, Keith won the nomination for Ed Whitcomb and Ed went on to a strong victory in the November election.

In hindsight, most of the players in that contest were winners. Bulen moved into state and national leadership positions in both political and civic organizations. Bowen later became Indiana's first governor to serve two consecutive terms, and Butz served five years as U.S. Secretary of Agriculture under Presidents Nixon and Ford (1971-1976).

Keith Bulen's positive leadership, on a variety of fronts, has helped to make both Indiana and the nation a wonderful place for all of us to live, to work, and to pursue happiness. There is no greater tribute to human endeavor than this.

Earl Butz is Dean Emeritus of Agriculture at Purdue University and he served as United States Secretary of Agriculture under Presidents Nixon and Ford.

I Liked His Style

by Orvas E. Beers

I served as the Allen County Republican Chairman from 1961 until 1993. During those 32 years, I became well acquainted with Keith Bulen and developed a very close friendship with him. The end result was a strong alliance between Marion and Allen Counties. Our friendship spread to include leaders in many of the other Indiana counties, and it made many of us more effective as Republican leaders. Politics during the "Bulen Era" was enjoyable and the successes were numerous. Keith's intelligence, ingenuity, ego, drive, and far-sightedness, were vital to the overall strength of the Indiana Republicans. He attracted many good cohorts such as John Sweezy, Mitch Daniels, Gordon Durnil, and a multitude of others who diligently worked to win elections with good candidates.

Keith Bulen's word was his bond. I liked him and I liked his style.

Orvas Beers is an attorney and a long time Republican leader from Northeastern Indiana.

How Candidates Are Nominated

As we change our calendars to the third millennium, we often breathe a sigh of relief when thirty percent of the voters participate in primary elections, a shameful showing. Voters complain about the quality of their office holders and say "there ain't a dime worth of difference between Republicans and Democrats," but they don't seem to care enough to help select the nominees of their party. Still, in the early 1970s, primary elections were promoted as a major political reform for the people. Prior to that time, most major office nominees were selected in convention and the reformers talked about smoked filled rooms. Open it up, they said. Let the people do it. We did and the people didn't. Political reform is often not a good thing—more often exclusive rather than inclusive.

It might well be time for an unbiased study determining the quality of candidates nominated in convention versus those nominated in primary elections. In his essay, Earl Butz refers to himself as a victim of the convention process, while Bob Orr was a beneficiary and owes much of his political career to the convention. Both honor the system, and both recognize Keith Bulen's adroit ability to work within the convention system. A comparison of the two systems, might be in order.

State Convention

In convention, the voters are people interested in who the candidates of the party should be. They subject themselves to an election process to earn the honor of serving as a delegate to a state political party convention. In essence, they care. They want their party to put forth the best and strongest candidate. Television advertising is not economical or effective with a only few thousand delegates. They meet the candidates personally, weigh the candidates' assets and liabilities, and cast a knowledgeable vote. How much money the candidate has is not the major consideration for nomination at a convention. How good of an office holder the candidate will be is a major consideration.

Primary Elections

Primary elections are usually preceded by stories in the news media predicting that few people will vote. Those predictions are usually self-fullfilling. Do primary voters vote for the strongest candidate or for the one whose name appears first on the ballot? Are such voters persuaded by what they know about the candidate, or by how they have been influenced by television commercials, positive and negative? How much money the candidate has to advertise is a major factor in determining nominees in a primary election.

In a democracy, the people should decide—ergo the populist promotion of primary elections. But ours is a democratic republic and James Madison feared the chaos of pure democracy. He, and our other founders, preferred a republican form of democracy where we elect people to represent us in congress, the legislature, or in convention. We have been taught to think otherwise, but isn't the convention system the most American? It's worth consideration.

Go For Broke

by Robert D. Orr

I first became acquainted with Keith Bulen as a fellow county chairman. I was Vanderburgh County Republican Chairman from 1965 to 1971, and I was able to observe firsthand his effective leadership of the Republican Action Committee as it took control of the Republican Party in Marion County. Suddenly, in June of 1972, I became a beneficiary of Keith's constructive leadership.

My tale describing Keith Bulen's greatly respected effectiveness as a political leader starts in far-off Southwestern Indiana. My home town of Evansville was also the home of incumbent Lieutenant Governor Dick Folz, who had called a meeting of local party leaders about three weeks before the State Republican Convention. I attended that meeting as an incumbent state senator, a candidate for re-election to a new four-year term, and as a retired county chairman.

Dick Folz was Governor Edgar D. Whitcomb's governmental teammate. Both were in the last year of a successful four year term. In those days, incidentally, governors were limited by the Indiana State Constitution to non-successive four year terms. In Evansville, we thought that Dick Folz was a logical and experienced choice to succeed Ed Whitcomb as governor—never mind that the very popular Otis R. "Doc" Bowen from far northern Indiana, and the Speaker of the House of Representatives, was expected to have a lock on the gubernatorial nomination.

With the nominating convention less than a month away, we presumed that the purpose of the home town meeting was for Dick Folz to rally support to win the nomination. We were eager to learn the roles we enthusiasts were to play at the convention to enable Folz to gain the nomination. Imagine our shock a few moments after assembling to hear Dick Folz tell us he would not be a candidate for governor. Instead, he planned to support Doc Bowen for governor, and then return to private life.

Folz didn't seem to hear our objections to his unexpected decision. After many decades of drought in respect to the presence of a southwestern area Hoosier in a key role in state government, we had found Folz's incumbency a very positive experience. To have him depart the scene of his own free will was tough to swallow. "Why?" But he was adamant. His mind was made up. Sadly, and as a likely explanation for his decision not to run, Dick Folz passed away a few months later of a heart attack. His doctor must have forewarned him.

At that same meeting, my county chairman Don Cox turned to me and said, "You've got to run for lieutenant governor. He was firm and convincing. Vice Chairman Bettye Lou Jerrel enthusiastically agreed. Soon the group decided a southern Indiana candidate was vital to the success of the ticket. My protestations were ignored. Overwhelmed as I was, I agreed to talk to my wife Josie, our children, and to my brother-business partner. Instead of expected resistance, the family reaction was strong for me to go ahead.

One day later we were engaged in a plan of action. The state convention was only three weeks away. Not much time to mount a campaign. My main job was to contact county chairmen and vice chairmen face to face throughout the state, because in those days the nomination for governor and lieutenant governor was decided in convention with 3,000 or so delegates casting votes. I had a lot of help from many home town friends and from numerous associates in the legislature. Having served as a county chairman from one of Indiana's largest counties for six years, I had the good fortune of knowing many of the chairmen and they knew me. Still, I had to convince them I would be a good candidate and try to gain their support. Television, so important now when we have direct primary elections to determine nominees, was of no value in my race. Politics then was a people to people business. I had to sell my cause to 92 county chairmen, 92 vice chairmen, a 22 member state committee, and eventually to the delegates. We did go "high tech" for those times, sending by UPS (in it's infancy) to all county chairs a tape player extolling my assets. The cost for that project was $7,000.

First on my list of personal contacts with county chairmen was L. Keith Bulen, Marion County's strong and savvy chairman. When I visited him, he asked a few typically straightforward questions seeking to determine the seriousness of my intentions. He seemed receptive. Despite the fact that John Hart, Chairman of the House Ways and Means Committee and a Marion County Republican, was already a candidate for lieutenant governor, Bulen told me right then and there that I would have the support of the Marion County delegation. His decision came quickly, clearly, and with no hesitation.

With Keith Bulen and Don Cox, the two best political leaders in Indiana and representing nearly one-half of the delegates needed for nomination on my side, I had all the encouragement I needed to go for broke. Over the next two weeks I burned rubber on Indiana highways from north to south, east to west, all across Indiana. I personally met with as many of the remaining ninety county chairs as possible, renewing friendships and enlisting support. The count was getting close, and I was beginning to think that my chances for success were good.

It was Keith Bulen's support of my candidacy that convinced many other, less committed, party leaders to swing my way. The day of the convention was the longest of my life, with three ballots taken before the nomination was mine. The second ballot was a killer, but between ballots Bulen and Cox were in the aisles and back rooms convincing other chairmen to go my way. They rounded up the votes necessary to push me over the top with a clear majority. Keith's skill, determination, and leadership, made the difference. I now realize that second ballot really determined my future: the immediate nomination for lieutenant governor, the responsibility to run independently as a statewide candidate (in those days the governor and lieutenant governor ran separately, not as a team as they now do), and the opportunity to serve two four year terms as Governor Bowen's partner. That prelude gave me the chance to be Indiana's governor for eight additional years, and opened the door for my later appointment as Ambassador to Singapore.

That quick decision at the eleventh hour by Keith Bulen abruptly changed my life and a bit of Indiana history as well. As I contemplate today this example of leadership, I conclude that the world would function better if all political or governmental leaders had the courage and common sense to make difficult decisions as firmly, decisively, and quickly, as Keith Bulen typically did throughout his lengthy and highly successful political experience. Selfishly, I am ever grateful for his key support for me beginning in that pivotal June of 1972.

Robert D. Orr served as Governor of the state of Indiana and as Ambassador to Singapore. He is a businessman who also served as Lieutenant Governor, state senator, and political leader from the township to the international levels.

Politics With Meaning

by John M. Mutz

On December 1, 1998, office holders, activists, party leaders, and campaign managers, gathered on the campus of Indiana University Purdue University Indianapolis to honor L. Keith Bulen and listen to nationally respected leaders and journalists analyze contemporary American politics. The event was the first annual Bulen Symposium On American Politics, made possible through an endowment of more than $100,000 created by 200 of Bulen's friends and former foes.

Why would so many veterans of the political system set up a fund to honor someone who has been out of the limelight for several years and never held a major elective office? The answer is not simple. It's partly because he has been one of the most effective local, state, and national leaders in Hoosier history. Among many other responsibilities, he served as Marion County GOP Chairman, Republican National Committeeman from Indiana, and key strategist in Ronald Reagan's victories. He pioneered the use of computerized, personalized direct mail in Indiana political campaigns and he initiated centralized call centers as a campaign technique. But most importantly it is because he represents a bygone era of patronage and party politics at its best. His approach to the political process doesn't really exist anymore and the current generation probably doesn't understand how it ever worked.

Partisan politics, practiced in the precincts during the first half of the 20th Century, was instrumental in the development of the most diverse nation on the face of the globe. For immigrants and minorities, working in local political organizations was one of the few ways to gain access to the mainstream of the American economy and society. But the reform movements of the fifties and sixties eliminated patronage and sapped the power of leaders like Bulen. Ironically, now society laments some of the very things that made the democratic system work in the past.

An *Indianapolis Star* article published in August of 1997 referred to Bulen as "crusty, cagey, and still connected." It even quoted me as saying "You either care about him or hate his guts. I happen to care about him." While everyone who knows him will admit that Keith was a complex personality, no one would doubt his belief that political movements make a difference in the outcome of human events and in the kind of progress enjoyed by our society.

During Bulen's tenure, a political movement that changed the face of government was the work of the Republican Action Committee started in 1965. Under Bulen's leadership, a group of young Republicans and a handful of Republican office holders decided that they could do it better than the old guard. They set about changing things by focusing on the most basic of political actions—the election of Republican precinct committeemen. In fact, the Action Committee in 1966 elected more than 225 committeemen in contested races. Seldom ever do you see a contest for committeemen. Today it's a struggle just to get people to do the job.

The grassroots political effort became the launching pad for Unigov in Marion County and the political careers of men and women such as Richard Lugar, Dan Burton, Bill Hudnut, Bill Ruckelshaus, Sue Anne Gilroy, Steve Goldsmith, Edgar Whitcomb, Marge O'Laughlin, Joyce Brinkman, John Mutz, and dozens of others.

But, more importantly, the political movement had meaning because it was aimed at creating a new level of competency in local government and a coordinated look at how urban government functions. In other words, it was the contention of the draftors of Unigov that the suburbs and the inner city were interrelated and their economic fortunes rose and fell together. This principle has served us well since 1969 when this historic legislation was passed in the Indiana General Assembly. Unigov has become the major building block that has turned Indianapolis into a competitor for major national attractions, including the Republican National Convention in 2000.

Bulen had an uncanny knack at motivating people in the precincts. He did it through a combination of charisma, charm, and the artful use of political influence. Jobs in government were made available under the old 2% club. When a person got a job through this process, two percent of the salary was pledged to the party in power.

Bulen's era was a time when license branches were privatized under the direction of the governor's political party. Although it's unlikely that we'll ever go back to the patronage system, it is important to occasionally recount some of the benefits of the practice. The patronage system provided party financing through lots of small contributions with very few large contributors, even though there were no campaign finance laws to limit large givers. The system insulated politicians from influence peddlers because the party organization stood between the lobby and the decision-maker.

Bulen not only knew how to motivate people in the precincts, he also knew how to make the patronage system work. He understood the two most important principles of how change takes place in our society: first with ideas and then with relationships. And L. Keith Bulen built the relationships that even to this day have an enormous influence on Marion County and our system of government.

Perhaps the legacy that Keith Bulen has left us all is not only the men and women he brought to public life, nor the ideas that he espoused and made real, but the belief that a strong party system may be the salvation of our democracy. At a time when money speaks, influence peddlers hold sway, and thirty second sound bits are the major ingredients of civil discourse, a return to party discipline and ideological difference could be a welcome change. It also could be an approach that would halt the spiraling cynicism that too many Americans today express about our political institutions.

John Mutz is a businessman who served as a State Representative, State Senator, and for two terms as Lieutenant Governor of the state of Indiana.

Working Magic

by Joan McNagny

My husband Bill and I have been supportive of the Republican Party since our marriage fifty years ago in 1949. Since then we have worked with Allen County Republican chairmen who were good organizers and knew how to "get out the vote."

Bill served as precinct committeeman, ward chairman, city attorney, and as an active member of the party finance committee. I canvassed neighborhoods for the Republican Party with a baby in a stroller, passed out doughnuts behind a baby elephant in a parade, been president of the Allen County Women's Republican Club, and in 1972 I was a co-chair of the Indiana Nixon Re-Elect Committee.

I mention all of this to show that I have been cognizant of the structure of the party and its leadership for many years. I've seen a lot, but in my opinion Keith Bulen was the finest political leader by far! Our country would be blessed if it had more like him. In the Nixon campaign, I watched him work his magic in decision-making, in the selection of candidates, and in fund-raising. I remember one day when we flew around Indiana on a fund-raising trip. His energy and commitment worked wonders.

If I had three wishes, one of them would be that we could clone Keith Bulen. Our country needs such dedication and ability.

Joan McNagny is a premier model for volunteerism, serving in politics, community affairs, charities, and professional organizations. She also served as President of the Indiana Lawyers Auxiliary and as President of the American Bar Association Auxiliary.

The Gonfalonier

by P. E. MacAllister

The history of a given era, event, person, incident is really shaped by how we remember or recollect it. Which suggests we not only re-call but apply our own personal judgment in the process as we reflect on its meaning or impact or ultimate effect. In ruminating on the life and times of L. Keith Bulen, there is no way I can avoid putting a personal "spin" on it, developed by my relationship with him, with the party, my views on what should happen and then what ultimately did happen and all of this not from the proximity of the "inner circle" but as a player a notch or two out on the periphery.

I first recall Keith as part of the Republican Action Committee, established very late 1964 and created to reconstruct and re-orient the Marion County Republican party. It was using the established process to take control of the machine from someone who had lost too many races, managed autocratically, represented the "party boss" style in such a fashion that he lost the support necessary to win of-fices. Since he was not interested in change, the only way to get our act together was to get a new chairman. And that is what the move-ment was all about, pretty much led by people who were non-office holders or professional politicians. The problem was evident, the need to control the party initiative was the objective with the vision of designing a better city the ultimate goal.

The fact that the Action Committee organized itself and told its story well and did indeed have the muscle to unseat the old guy is history. But in achieving that, all would have been an exercise in treadmilling if we could not find the right person to assume control of the apparatus and deploy it in a fashion that would result in better governance, better service, ultimately a better city. So Keith was the key. He was the second phase of the whole effort; i.e. first generate support so we can run the show and then, second find someone to drive the bloody machine. Because if we don't properly manage what we have gained, we have benefited no one. So he was the point man, the gonfalonier and he was duly elected County Chairman, assuming the office and the responsibility.

The other aspect to this given time and place was the abundance of young people, then graduating from the ranks of the Young Republicans, who were dying for a chance to play a role in the democratic institutions of the republic, especially those at local and state levels. People like Jim Morris, Dick Lugar, Ned Lamkin, John Mutz, Tom Hasbrook, Dan Burton, Bill Ruckelshaus, Marge O'Laughlin, Larry Borst, to name a few. Unless we were able to win elections, these folks would never surface on the political scene, given the Democratic majority. The only way to give our people a shot was to be better organized, better funded, supply better candidates, do a better job in the precincts and wards and generally outsmart them. And, of course, to do that, we had to have the cerebral acuity as well as the passion or design along with good intentions. We had to have someone who could keep it all organized and effectuate a strategy which the Action Committee had envisioned. We had to find a guy like Keith Bulen.

Which means an action person. Keith occasionally might have been wrong, but he was never in doubt. He was positive, visionary, decisive, intelligent, experienced, informed and appropriately autocratic. I mean, he didn't have to call a lot of meetings to make decisions. He was an inspiration to the ward and precinct people; was a good strategist when it came to running campaigns; good in looking at numbers; a good teacher and tactician. At a point in time when it was all coming together, he was the ideal person for the job since he had a can-do sort of attitude. Then too, he worked well with the whole team. He also had the gift of telling you what he thought, but left you alone to do what you knew was right.

In retrospect, what we did in those days was change the entire course and direction of the city of Indianapolis and we did it because we had the capacity to find good people like Lugar and Mills and Borst and SerVaas and Hudnut and then the strength to run campaigns that got them elected so their talent could be applied to enhancing the fame and glory of 'ole Indy.' Key to all of that, to putting it all together, was of course L. Keith Bulen. In so doing, he helped us get Indianapolis on the map, changed the quality of government, the physical profile of the city, the competence of appointed boards and agencies, the attitude of people about their city. In the results of his leadership and achievement he has left a legacy from which even the next generations will benefit substantially.

P.E. MacAllister, Chairman of the Board of MacAllister Machinery, Inc., is a long time civic, political, business, and church leader with The Indiana Opera Theatre being one of his success stories.

Once Upon A Time

by Dr. Beurt R. SerVass

Once upon a time, when I was early into Marion County politics, I was persuaded by one of the many factions opposing Republican County Chairman Dale Brown (covertly) to run against him (as a sacrificial lamb) to "test the waters." Donald Bruce, then a Congressman, was the pied piper coaxing me to run just two days before the county convention. I lost, of course, but I came to the attention of one Keith Bulen who took me to his office after the election and told me to "take it on the chin." It is this sort of thing, he confided, that "builds character!"

I recovered from this defeat and later was slated to run for County Council. I won the second time. Then came a split on the seven-member council when we were to re-appoint a particular odious member of the liquor board. Dale Brown owned three members of the council, including the then council president. Noble Pearcy, the county prosecutor, controlled three council members and he opposed Dale's choice 110%. I diligently tried to bridge the breach, even making a three day trip to Miami, where Dale instructed me how to bet "intelligently" and to win consistently betting only on horses to win, place and show.

After Dale lost a few races (he only bet small change), I got him to shift the subject to the liquor board appointments. He was adamant that his Democrat attorney be reappointed and said he would count on me. I responded that we would appoint any "body" in Marion County other than his current Democrat. Dale then replied for the 10th time, "he's the only one, Beurt." So, I went home.

The next day Noble Pearcy came to my office to get the "good word." "Noble" I said, "if I vote for you it will definitely split the party. It won't be the same again. The day after we reject Dale, he will definitely read us out of favor and there will be no returning."

I voted to appoint Pearcy's candidate and a total of thirteen current office holders and important appointees (including me) were "disowned" by Dale Brown, and we were thence forth on our own.

The split was complete and did not heal. So our small group had no plausible alternative but to organize into a not so "loyal" opposition, which I hopefully suggested be called The Republican Action Committee. Circuit Court Judge John Niblack nominated himself to be the chair of the committee, but I persuaded the rest to include a prominent "non-governmental figure" which I suggested should be John Burkhart. After some raucous discussion, it was done.

I also proposed that I try to raise $100,000 to contest the next precinct committeeman election. With a faint heart, the committee agreed and appointed me treasurer and chief financial officer. John Burkhart, then immediate past chairman of the Chamber of Commerce and president of College Life Insurance Company, was in no position to be an active chair and so the committee launched a search for a "working chairman." Keith Bulen offered his full time services, but he was vigorously opposed by Pearcy and Marcia Hawthorne, the County Recorder, and by a few others. Keith's candidacy did not prosper, at which time, I received the only invitation, ever, to a paid lunch by "candidate Bulen" to be held in a "neutral" place—the Indianapolis Athletic Club, so we could discuss common interests.

During lunch, Keith proposed that I be his campaign manager and turn this committee around by assuring the RAC members that here was a "brass knuckles" motivated chairman candidate that could win enough precincts to elect a county chairman and start a winning campaign for the whole Republican ticket.

The key thing to remember here is that (1) Keith did pay for the lunch, and (2) Keith actually thought I could do it and asked me to be his "campaign manager." Subsequent events did cause Noble and Marsha to back down and Keith went on to create a great deal of success and controversy and good humor in these parts, including huge victories at the polls and some good government to boot.

I am still the treasurer of the Party which doesn't mean much these days as candidates soak up most all available funds.

Dr. Beurt SerVaas is the long-time president of the Indianapolis City-County Council and a successful businessman.

Occasionally Irascible

by James T. Neal

Keith Bulen may or may not have liked smoke-filled rooms, but when the smoke cleared he was always in command. He did like dedication and hard work, which he himself provided. For those traits he got loyalty from his followers and respect from his peers.

Keith was the last effective political "boss" of the 20th Century in Indiana. In fact, he may have been the most able political leader in the post-Vietnam era across the nation. He elected city council members, mayors, legislators, governors, senators, and helped to elect presidents. But equally important, Keith always had a sense of history. He was not in politics for power alone but for what power could do to improve government—and the Republican Party. He was far-sighted and innovative, whether creating an effective party apparatus, defining a united county government, or bringing nations together as he was able to do in resolving problems between the United States and Canada.

Occasionally irascible, often demanding and impatient, Keith had no patience for pedestrian politics. His operations were giant-sized and in living technicolor. He displayed his shortcomings and his achievements with equal zeal, all the while challenging his friends' reactions to both. In a word, he had "chutzpah." It made the Bulen era, if sometimes unpredictable, always exciting.

Party politics have changed since Keith moved into the shadows. No longer do political parties motivate the electorate, who are more interested in the personalities of individual candidates, or in specific issues—or not interested at all. Like the smoke-filled rooms, the good old days in politics will not come back. The Bulens who led us to so many victories are now history. How unfortunate for America.

Jim Neal was the long time publisher of The Noblesville Ledger *newspaper. He served as Indiana Republican State Chairman (1972-1974) and as Indiana's National Committeeman on the Republican National Committee.*

Supermarket Wine

by Robert Novak

Keith Bulen is one of those rare politicians that a political reporter enjoys spending time with even if he does not always get much in the way of hard facts—a category of politician in unfortunately short supply these days.

Back in the early '70s, I once compared notes with Johnny Apple of *The New York Times* about who we would most like to be with to partake of a steak and a good bottle of wine. Keith Bulen was very high on the list. Keith often seemed to us to be more of a journalist than a politician, and that is meant as a compliment. By this, I mean that his B.S. content was extremely low and his ability to scent out political poseurs was extraordinary. His humor was cutting without being vicious, and it was often turned against journalists. It's hard to exaggerate how different Keith seemed compared to the normal run of Republican pols—especially in the Nixon era.

Bulen was a serious politician, deeply immersed in the great party issues over a long period of time. I think he failed in his greatest project—to position Dick Lugar to be President of the United States—no easy venture, to be sure. But he could be delighted by simple pleasures. I remember how delighted he was in his new Indianapolis office with a wet bar, describing it (tongue firmly in cheek as it often was): "This fulfills my greatest lifetime ambition."

One small anecdote. Keith and his wife were our guests at dinner in our Maryland suburban home long ago. My wife, Geraldine, in an unprecedented initiative toward economy, decided she had had enough of guests not appreciating expensive wine and leaving their glasses half full. So, she bought cheap but certainly drinkable supermarket wine, emptied the bottles and put it in carafes. Of course, nobody would notice—or would not say anything if he did notice. But Keith took a sip, turned to my wife and said: "Ah, Geraldine. Excellent! I always say you can get excellent wine at the supermarket!"

You couldn't fool Keith Bulen on matters small or large, and he would let you know if you were trying to fool him.

Bob Novak is a journalist who has covered national politics at the highest levels. He is probably best known as a syndicated columnist for the Chicago Sun-Times *and his television work on* Evans & Novak, Crossfire *and much more.*

For All The Right Reasons

by Muriel D. Coleman

The 1980 Republican National Convention was the first time the country would get a good look at Ronald Reagan. It was of paramount importance that his national campaign be given a good sendoff, so to lead the convention effort the Reagan team tapped a man from Indiana. A political legend, the Reagan folks must've thought him a superman, because they gave him only one staff member—me. He knew better and brought the Hoosiers with him.

He walked into my office one day in May carrying a briefcase with two people tagging behind. I rose from behind my desk as he smiled and said, "I'm Keith Bulen from Indiana." I had met a legend and he had met his deputy. In less than two months we would organize the convention that would nominate Ronald Reagan for President of the United States. Keith was confident. I was not.

I wasn't a novice in politics. I had run a number of campaigns in Wisconsin: as a youth I organized my state Young Republicans into a 5,000 member fighting force during the antiwar days of Vietnam, and I even tried my hand as a candidate for public office. I worked for both the Speaker of our State Assembly, Harold Froehlich, and then Assistant Minority Leader, Tommy Thompson. I served on our state GOP committee where I chaired many political events. But here I was at age 35 dedicating myself to make certain America was strong. I had confidence in my abilities, but I was uncertain that my abilities matched the needs of Keith Bulen. I was about to find out.

I talked with three people on the national Reagan staff about Keith, and it was Jim Stockdale who told me, "When you become friends with Keith Bulen, you have a friend for life." That spring 1980 day in Detroit the acorn of friendship was planted and it became a towering oak.

The national convention was an official function of the Republican National Committee, but since Governor Reagan had enough delegates to win nomination on the first ballot, it became the Reagan convention. So what we planned became important not just for the

20,000 delegates, reporters, and guests of the convention, but for millions of voters watching on television. Our offices were in the Renaissance Center in downtown Detroit. Keith and I shared a rather small office with our desks at right angles. Early on he said, "I'm giving you the toughest jobs of the convention—tickets and housing—and you'll be third in charge of everything else. We will monitor each other's telephone calls so both of us will know what's going on." The scope of the job was beginning to dawn on me. Heading up housing and tickets meant that I would be saying "no" to a lot of people, even people of importance.

Keith's reasons for confidence were twofold: First he knew what needed to be done to have a successful convention, and second he brought people from Indiana to implement his plan. The chief "budgeteer" was Fred Armstrong, Comptroller for the city of Indianapolis—a walking-talking computer who knew all details of our budget. His assistant, CPA Bill Trinkle, would join us later.

So we could communicate with one another, Keith brought Tom Allebrandi of Carmel. One Sunday, Tom built a base station atop our center so we could receive our own frequency that he obtained from the FCC. The most envied duties were the ones to which Keith assigned a "walkie-talkie" or beeper. The transportation fleet was managed by the unflappable Lee Richardson. We had more than 40 cars, RVs, vans, and trailers to move V.I.P.s from once place to another. The security team of 12 Indianapolis police officers was headed up by the vigilant Don Christ. They took vacation time to protect the national Reagan staff for Keith. Secured RVs were positioned outside Cobo Hall with fencing around them to protect the candidate and staff. Whenever I had tickets in my possession, an armed guard was with me.

The medical team was headed by Marion County Coroner Dr. Dennis Nicholas. He was joined by Dr. Ben Clayburgh of North Dakota and four nurses. The social chairman was Warren Spangle of the Indiana Restaurant Association. He organized the delegate reception the night before the convention which resembled "A Taste Of Detroit." Warren also planned our nightly dinners, because I was to learn that dinner was merely an extension of the work day. When

Warren's son joined us, we often heard "Spangle to Spangle" on the walkie-talkies.

Keith printed and distributed a newspaper to delegates every day, in the midst of a newspaper strike going on in Detroit. Delegates were greeted each morning at their Michigan and Canadian hotels with a Reagan newspaper under their door. The editor was a bright young attorney from Indianapolis named Peter Rusthoven. Bill Colbert was in charge of distribution.

Fourteen hundred kids showed up to be part of the convention experience and stayed at Ypsilanti University forty miles from Detroit. Donna Tuttle from California was the youth coordinator. She was assisted by Dan Dean from Michigan, who reminded us that his future was a big reason that we were working for Ronald Reagan. Another Michigander, Andrea Fischer, became my assistant, and her computer skills saved the day for us on several occasions. Other primary Michigan contacts were State Chairman John Gnau, Finance Chairman Bob Chambers, and GOP Executive Director, Terry Davis—all extremely helpful.

The month of June saw more Hoosiers joining us. Ruby Miller was Keith's political secretary, and Anne Schuster a key volunteer. Nancy Harris from Massachusetts joined the team as did numerous friends from other states. But when Keith needed a task performed, he would make a beeline for the Hoosiers whom he knew and trusted, and they were already trained. Keith was a big picture kind of guy. He made sure that everyone who helped Ronald Reagan get the nomination were recognized at the convention. The Ten Club, chaired by Mary Jane Wick of California, was given a special reception and passes to the convention.

No detail was too small to care about. Keith wanted to know what our balloons for the big balloon drop were going to cost. When he was told the price, he found a volunteer to drive a truck to California to pick up the balloons at a saving of $1,000. As noon approached on my first day on the job I got up and Keith asked where I was going. "To lunch," I said. He said he didn't eat lunch and I said, "I do." Stalemate. So I told him that I didn't eat breakfast and I was hungry. I went out and brought back a cheeseburger and root beer to eat at my desk. From then on, every single day, Bill Colbert brought me a cheeseburger and root beer from McDonalds. It was also from Bill Colbert that I learned that Keith thought so fast he left words out of his sentences. You had to supply the missing words yourself.

While worrying about the national convention, Keith was also a practicing attorney. Several times each week I called his law office to get messages. One day I was told, "Wuv is in foal." She repeated it twice for me, but I asked, "What is Wuv?" I was then told about his horses. Wuv was one of his horses and the secretary volunteered to send a list of his 40 horses so I could be knowledgeable about them. I said, "No, thanks. I have enough on my plate." We worked 16-22 hours a day to get ready for the convention. To give us a break, Keith flew us to Ohio to watch one of his horses race. Returning to Detroit, I mentioned how beautiful the Ren-Cen was from the air. Keith had the pilot fly around until John Gnau and Terry Davis became dizzy. If you mentioned something that you liked to Keith, he tried to give it to you.

One night I went to dinner with Keith and the "boys," and after dinner Keith told me that we would sacrifice everything to get Ronald Reagan elected—"for all the right reasons." I told him there was one price I couldn't pay. I had gone into false blindness three times before and I promised myself that I would not sacrifice my eyes. He understood, and every morning thereafter he would ask, "How are your eyes?" In chatting with the Hoosiers who were there at their own expense, I told them how fortunate Ronald Reagan was to have their support. To a person, they said they were doing it for Keith. And no one worked harder than Keith. It was almost impossible to keep up with him and to meet his high standards. He expected the best from himself and we all tried to give our best.

Throughout May, June, and July, we worked on a small budget to launch our candidate to victory. The hours were grueling. The pressures intense—both inside the campaign and in meeting outside requests. The care of 5,000 delegates was no small task, but on the night of July 16th, in the midst of a marvelous red, white, and blue, balloon drop, Ronald Reagan was nominated. George Bush was his choice for Vice President. In two weeks, we all went our separate ways.

Keith Bulen as a boss was tenacious, honest, caring, piercing, loyal, brilliant, overbearing, overindulging, opinionated, brusque, compassionate, detail-oriented, suave, cultured, intense, inspiring, dedicated, demanding, fair, flamboyant, personal, emotional, mature, and my friend. His was a multidimensional personality, and he would criticize you in one breath and lead you to greatness in another. If you shot back when he seemed insulting, you were going to miss his real point. I went from amazement at all he knew and had accomplished, to sheer frustration when he assumed that I could accomplish complex tasks in short periods of time. I learned from him that when I was so exhausted that I could cry, I still had at least two or three good, productive hours in me to give to the cause. No matter how exhausted, our leader was there with us.

Ronald Reagan was elected in November. Taxes were cut. Our national defenses rebuilt. America took on a new pride and the Soviet Union imploded. We contributed to all of those good events. I am glad Jim Stockdale talked me into working on the Reagan campaign and glad that Charlie Black sent me to Michigan to work with Keith. I never knew if I contributed sufficiently to warrant his approval, except Keith did ask me to stay on for the fall campaign on the eastern desk. I didn't. I stayed in the midwest and I have worked for myself ever since. Keith was my last boss. No one else could measure up.

Ronald Reagan often talked about a shining city on a hill. One of the guiding lights to that city was L. Keith Bulen of Indiana.

Muriel D. Coleman (Bucky) is a conservative political consultant and the owner of a year around Christmas and yarn store in Madison, Wisconsin.

Encourager

by Nat Hill, IV

When a person is highly successful in his endeavors, people use many different words to describe that person. Keith Bulen was a highly successful man and has been described using many different words, such as: successful, arrogant, caring, egomaniacal, relentless, motivator, charismatic, articulate, grumpy, and the list goes on. The word that comes to my mind is "encourager."

Keith Bulen owned perhaps the most successful sire in the history of harness racing. Keith's involvement in harness racing was always been strong, but never more so than when he finally quit electing presidents and passing laws. I have been quite active in promoting Standardbred causes, but freely admit I have neither the skills or connections to make anywhere near the contributions that Keith has over the years. Horsemen are a difficult group to work with, and my view of the industry was—and is—often at odds with horsemen in general and often with Keith Bulen in particular.

It is a sign of the character of this man, that in spite of our frequent disagreements, he always encouraged me. We communicated through e-mail and in person on numerous occasions. Keith was never been too busy to talk to me. At the times in my life when my efforts seemed to be the least appreciated and I begin to wonder if it is all worth the effort, Keith Bulen, a man who elected Presidents, always found the time to encourage Nat Hill, a man who couldn't elect himself to the student council.

I doubt that Keith understood how honored I was that he took time out of his hectic life to "minister" to me in his own special style. At one particularly low point in my efforts to help horsemen, I wrote a very petulant letter to Keith. His response was a classic, and I wish to share part of it here. I quite literally keep these as words to live by.

From Keith Bulen:

Nat—I've spent a lifetime doing for others and causes what they can't or don't do or deserve on their own. Keeping one's word is a beautiful and honorable major feat that is only self satisfying. So what else is there in the long, long race?

LKB

There isn't much else "in the long, long race." Keith Bulen was an encourager, and a man I was honored to call friend.

Nat Hill IV graduated from Purdue University as a veterinarian, and is an assistant professor in the School of Medical Technology at the IU Med Center. Nat's family has been in the harness racing business for well over fifty years, and Keith Bulen's first venture into harness racing was as a co-owner with Nat's late father, Judge Nat U. Hill of Bloomington. His mother, Margie, served on the Republican State and National committees with Keith Bulen. Nat Hill IV serves on the Standardbred Breed Development Advisory Committee. He owns and races trotters at Hoosier Park and Indiana county fairs.

Stay Out Of Indiana

by Donald L. Totten

My first recollection of Keith Bulen is from the 1980 Reagan campaign. One of my states to supervise was Indiana. Keith's response to my offer to help was, "Stay out of Indiana. We know how to run a campaign."

As I got to know Keith and his beloved state of Indiana, I came to realize the impact he has had on Republican politics there. His old fashioned "nuts and bolts" approach coupled with a belief that "to the victor belongs the spoils," enabled Keith to influence and help to build one of the most powerful and respected state party organizations in the country.

We served together on the International Joint Commission where I continued to develop a new respect for his command of issues and his "take charge" attitude. I became aware, as those in Indiana before me, that Keith Bulen had both the authority, leadership, and political intuition to successfully complete any task.

Don Totten is an engineer and a long-time national Republican leader from Illinois. He was appointed by President Ronald Reagan as a Commissioner on the International Joint Commission—United States and Canada.

Citizen Diplomat

by Glenn A. Olds

We met first in Geneva, Switzerland. He and I were both early Nixon appointees, I as Ambassador to the United Nation's Economic & Social Council and he as the President's lay delegate to our first meeting. Keith was recently married, seeking to combine his civic responsibility with his personal honeymoon.

Housing was tight and expensive, but the embassy had arranged, at his request, a suite at the Inter-Continental Hotel, but without a kitchenette or facilities. In spite of what I came to learn was Keith's generous disposition, and abiding concern for others, the arrangement was not quite satisfactory. The embassy officer, who met Keith and his wife, sensed that Keith was not pleased. When we met that evening at our apartment with my wife's first successful Swiss souffle, I was delighted to learn that Keith had cheerily forgotten his arrival and first introduction to Switzerland and, like a race horse, he was chomping at the bit to get started.

I asked Keith to take to lunch the ambassador seated next to us at the ECOSOC round table, a brilliant young Sorbonne graduate in law, who was from the Upper Volta in Africa. Keith was noticeably shaken by the number and quality of black ambassadors and I was eager to dispel his fears. I had the feeling he thought they were just out of cannibalism. Two hours after that first lunch, I remember his astonished look and exclamation, "My God, Olds," he said. "This guy knows more about Indianapolis than I do!" This was Keith's introduction to that wider world, which he took to like a duck to water.

His curiosity and interest were matched only by his competence. When I asked him to take the chairman's seat, as was my custom, he participated like an old pro—thoughtful, sensitive, and with rare diplomatic skill. His candor and openness endeared him to the other ambassadors. He shattered many of the then pro-Communist, anti-American capitalist images at the United Nations by being an honest, outgoing American capitalist genuinely interested in them, and in the world's problems. He became early sought after as a luncheon colleague, and I suspect, he did more to correct the rash and irresponsible views of our country than almost anyone else.

At the end of that session, Keith rented one of the fine chateau restaurants outside of Geneva, and invited every delegate and all of their support staff, the first time the latter had ever been done. The secretaries, chauffeurs, and staff people came to mix and mingle with the ambassadors, an American ideal as natural as apple pie, but never before witnessed in diplomatic circles.

When Keith began his final remarks, with such sensitivity and integrity, he broke down—and the whole assembly rose with resounding cheers. He came as an anonymous Midwestern lawyer. He left, an international hero, and an unforgettable American citizen-diplomat, which is what our country is all about. His conservatism remained staunch and absolutely dependable; but what he sought to conserve and practice was the American dream at its best, where every person is cherished as unique, equal, and deserving to be heard and served.

Keith remains for me, what the American political system is all about, mirror in miniature, of government of, by, and for, the people.

Glenn A. Olds has his PhD in philosophy and has been a teacher, President of Kent State University, Chairman of the World Federalist Association, and among many other things, U.S. Ambassador to the United Nations, 1969-1971.

Keith Never Suffered Fools Gladly

by Robert S. K. Welch, Q.C.

One of the many pleasures surrounding my time as a member of the International Joint Commission representing Canada was to meet and work with Keith Bulen, who was then serving on the commission at the pleasure of President Ronald Reagan. The two of us immediately struck up a meaningful and lasting friendship, even though our actual contact was not frequent after leaving the commission.

As we were becoming friends, I found it delightful to learn about Keith's successful political activities. I particularly enjoyed conversing with an individual who held strong views based on conviction and principle, and I was never left in doubt about where Keith Bulen stood on any issue of importance. We shared a mutual interest in politics and in the work of the International Joint Commission. His recognition of the responsibilities we have as stewards of our natural resources resulted in a keen interest in matters of the environment and balanced development. He also taught me a great deal about negotiation and mediation.

Keith never suffered fools gladly. There are many who carry the scars to prove that statement true. No doubt there were those who saw him as a crusty and difficult individual to deal with, but behind that appearance I found a warm, caring, and loyal, individual who, although firm, was consistently friendly and fair.

Robert S. K. Welch, former Deputy Premier of the Province of Ontario, represented Canada on the International Joint Commission; Chancellor, University of Brock in St. Catharines, Ontario.

Eeyore With An Attitude

by David LaRoche

Father of the modern Indiana Republican Party. Godfather to the Party's notables—Lugar, Ruckelshaus, Roudebush, Bowen, Orr. Confidante of Presidents. Reagan's Deputy Campaign Director, Director of the Republican National Convention in Detroit, and senior member of the Reagan Transition Team. Mike, a Carter Administration appointee to the International Joint Commission, United States and Canada (IJC), was rattling off Keith Bulen's credentials in awe and resignation.

"Unless there are two Keith Bulens out there, and it's true that he actually wants to come to this nowhere Commission, I may as well pack my bags now," he said.

That was my initial, if second-hand, introduction to Keith Bulen. I was also skeptical about the incoming Reagan appointees. Unlike Mike, I was a career official at the IJC and knew that it would be difficult for any new political appointees to have me fired. On the other hand, they could certainly isolate me and/or I could find myself surrounded by political hacks with little or no appreciation of the subtleties of the IJC and its promise, and watch an institution that I cared about become a comfortable perch for pols to conveniently foray into the muddle of beltway politics.

Meeting Keith Bulen firsthand was perplexing. Yes, there was only one Keith Bulen, and he was all of the things that I had been told. He was also impeccably dressed, polite, curious, and respectful. In that first meeting, and during the eight years that I worked with Keith at the IJC, partisanship was never an issue. I felt I owed it to Keith to share with him my political history—former administrative assistant to a Democratic U.S. Senator, State Chairman and Executive Director of the New Hampshire Democratic Party, in short—I was a liberal Democrat. It didn't matter. In fact, I think he was pleased that I was not ignorant of the political world, and he knew well that if this little commission were to have an influence on the U.S.-Canada relationship, political skills were an imperative.

During that first meeting, Keith did what Keith does best, he asked questions, lots of them. He was hungry to know how the Commission worked, what it had done well, what it had not done well or at all, what kinds of things made sense for future emphasis. Keith saw himself as a visionary. He wanted to do special things, things bigger than himself that would live far beyond the time that he had been involved with them. He brought those characteristics to the IJC. And he did, of course, bring all of those other quirky, sometimes difficult, always intense, Keith Bulen characteristics along for the ride.

After my initial interviews with Keith, and after getting through the mountains of paperwork he had to fill out to become a commissioner on the part of the United States, I met him in the main lobby of the State Department for his orientation. The orientation was to begin at 9:30 AM. He wanted to meet in the lobby at 9:00 AM. When I arrived at 9:04 AM Keith was alternately looking at his watch and gauging my approach. When I was comfortably within earshot he said simply "Next to timeliness, Godliness is an important virtue." Thus began my education in the complexities of this man, the roller coaster ride between his extremes of kindness and perversity, hope and despair, toughness and remarkable vulnerability.

Keith Bulen was in some ways the personification of Eeyore. He was convinced that if there was a little black cloud anywhere, it would find him, and then it would rain like hell: that if anything bad could happen it would, and that unless he was careful, unless he managed every last detail, the bad thing would happen to him. It's the careful part that separated Keith from Eeyore. Put another way, he was Eeyore with an attitude. Yes, lots of bad things happen to people, but if you plan diligently, leave nothing to chance, all of those bad things will happen to other people, hopefully your enemies. This insistence on leaving nothing to chance constantly surprised IJC staff meeting planners.

On the eve of the first major IJC conference of Keith's tenure, he stunned the planners by asking if they had yet recruited an emergency physician specifically for the conference. Was this a joke? The meeting was in Washington for God's sake. There are thousands of physicians in Washington, not to mention state-of-the-art emergency rooms in first class hospitals. It wasn't a joke, and when the planners eventually recruited the doc and presented the name address and phone number, Keith carried it a step further by insisting they find a back-up. "What if you call him and he's not there?"

There were times, though, when all of Keith's good planning could not help him. It was almost as though Providence acted forcefully to remind him of his fallibility. I remember one conference when Keith and I were the last to leave. It was winter. He had a lined, tan trench coat. There was one remaining tan trench coat on the rack. Keith put it on. It was unlined. The shoulders of the coat reached halfway down his arms. It fell to his ankles. With the sort of resigned look that I came to know as uniquely Keith, he said simply, "David, do you notice anything peculiar about this coat?"

Our first long trip was to Vancouver. We then drove from Vancouver to the Osoyoos valley in British Columbia, along the British Columbia-Washington State boundary noted for its fruit and wine production. The IJC had jurisdiction of a transboundary dam that controlled outflows from Osoyoos Lake in Canada into the Similkameen River in Washington. It is a dry part of the world where the value of scarce surface water rivals that of gold. We were there to inspect the dam and hold public hearings on what a new dam should take into account in the way of outflows. While Keith didn't say it, I knew that he expected to see a dam the size of a Hoover or Grand Coulee. This was Big Sky country after all, home to the legendary Big Dams of the 1950s—the intent of which was to provide irrigation for the new Garden of Eden and cheap power for all. And what else would justify all this time and expense?

In fact, the so-called Zosel Dam was an itty-bitty thing with wooden planks no more than three feet above the water, weathered chains snaking through rusted eyelets pretending to be a rail-guard, the whole thing vibrating noisily as the rushing water threatened to obliterate any evidence that there ever had been a dam. And with Keith's vision of his mighty dam disappearing he turned to me and asked, his voice quavering in sync with the strong vibration, "David, are you sure this is the right dam?"

It was on this western trip that Keith saw the promise for the commission to do something special for U.S.-Canada relations. It involved a separate dam. The city of Seattle and the province of British Columbia had been quarreling over Seattle's plans to raise the Ross Dam on the U.S. side of the boundary that would consequently flood thousands of acres of recreational land in British Columbia's Skagit River valley. The dam was 540 feet high already, almost the height of two football fields, a dam of truly Bulenesque proportions with or without the proposed 122 foot addition. And the disagreement between the city and the Province had been acrimonious enough to have captured the notice of both federal governments, at least to the extent to conclude it was an argument to be avoided. Even better, the IJC retained so-called continuing jurisdiction over the dam and thus could conceivably broker an agreement that would end the dispute.

Thus began a three year odyssey that would bring into a play all of Keith's skills—his ability to make everyone feel that they were something bigger than themselves, his ability to plan, negotiate, scold, outrage, charm, confuse (purposefully), and, ultimately, his indefatigable drive to prevail.

The Ross Dam controversy was a Gordian Knot laced with political, economic, and environmental threads. The original 540-foot dam had been built during the 1930s. But Seattle's plan to increase its height by 122 feet was not approved by the IJC until 1942, an approval that Seattle required because the heightened dam would flood into BC. The IJC was responsible, under the treaty between the United States and Canada, to "see to the indemnification of affected interests" that might exist on the other side of the national boundary. The IJC handled this by requiring that British Columbia and Seattle identify those affected interests on the Canadian side and make provision for indemnification. An agreement was finally arrived at in 1967, and was immediately assailed in BC as having been a sellout to the Americans, always a political winner in Canada, and the emergence of environmental considerations on both sides of the border. The political opposition to the raising of the dam was so strong in Canada that the government that signed the agreement was defeated, in part, because of its agreement support. And the new government, recognizing that it could attract support from across the border, encouraged the environmental objections as a way of getting the IJC to rescind its Order of Approval for raising the dam.

The situation inherited by Keith and his five colleagues on the IJC (the IJC is comprised of three Presidential appointees on the U.S. side and three Prime Ministerial appointees from Canada), which by precedent act only by consensus on such issues, seemed bleak. British Columbia had signed a legally binding agreement that it no longer intended to honor. Seattle had technical authority to raise its dam but knew that by doing so it would create an international incident and enrage the significant and growing number of environmental activists, many of whom were key constituents to Seattle political office holders. Both federal governments wanted the problem to go away, but had more of an interest in posturing than in asserting any leadership.

The Boundary Waters Treaty of 1909 between the US and Canada is a very interesting document. It created the IJC, and its Purpose is to prevent disputes along the common boundary. Keith had come to understand the power of this dispute prevention role and had recognized how it could be creatively used to get the city and the province back to the negotiating table to resolve the dispute amicably. British Columbia wanted the IJC simply to annul its Order of Approval to raise the dam in the name of "changed environmental values." Seattle wanted the commission to simply honor what it had originally decreed in 1942, terms which had been satisfied by the 1967 agreement. But Keith knew that the result of taking either of those courses would be to create a dispute along the common boundary, an action that arguably would be contrary to the spirit and letter of the Treaty.

The mayor of Seattle, Charlie Royer, and several ministers from British Columbia were invited to come to Washington to meet with the commission. Keith had managed to convince his colleagues that he and one Canadian commissioner should be given "lead" responsibility to deal with the issue in its entirety, thereby reducing the difficulty of convincing six different people of the relative merits of every decision point that would occur during the difficult negotiations. In the small IJC conference room, Seattle and BC were told, in a brief opening statement, that the IJC did not want to declare a winner and a loser. The responsible thing for them to do would be to help configure a win-win scenario to end the dispute, and, that if they could not do that, the commission would know who was largely responsible for the breakdown in negotiations and clearly implied that, notwithstanding the nationality interests on the commission, the responsible party would lose. The commission then withdrew and put their challenge to the first test—Seattle and BC were to remain in the room until they had decided to participate or not in commission led negotiations where, in the end, the commission would be de-facto arbitrator. Later, Seattle and BC negotiators would tell us that until that day they had no intention of dealing with each other, but they quickly decided that dealing with each other was preferable to dealing with this baffling, unpredictable commission.

Keith and his colleague, Ontario lawyer Richmond Olson, devised a Joint Consultative Group for the negotiations. They chaired the group. Keith was exceedingly businesslike, disciplined, and, as usual, frighteningly organized. Richmond was totally unpredictable. Bright and irascible, he spent the first several minutes of one important meeting in BC scolding the government for having arranged a meeting room with no windows. He would fairly regularly launch into near indecipherable philosophical musings about topics that seemed totally unrelated to the negotiation. You couldn't predict Richmond's behavior over the next five minutes, and his vote, if it came to that, was certainly unpredictable.

The negotiations were exceedingly complex. The key question to be resolved was how much power the additional 122 foot addition to the Ross Dam would yield over the period of its projected life, which was to the year 2066. Keith thinks big. He suggested the commission hire the former CEOs of Ontario Hydro and the then Power Authority of the State of New York to calculate the increment. The commission asked that Seattle and BC give them access to the files and records of Seattle City Light and BC Hydro. In the context of the implied threat, neither dared refuse. The process nearly broke down on several occasions, and each time Keith would remind the negotiators that they had to make sacrifices, that there was only one safe way out, and that both were responsible to the higher interests of the interests of both countries. Richmond would muse mysteriously, at times incoherently. No one save Keith could have kept Richmond even remotely targeted. They fed off each other. Keith had a genuine fascination for the understandable and even inscrutable parts of Richmond's genius, and Richmond knew that Keith was his ticket to ever succeeding in the non-abstract world, something I suspect that he had never accomplished to that point in his life. In the end, the negotiators would look baffled, then frightened, and then break through to the next level.

The basis of the agreement they reached was based on the objective of the joint construction of a "dam" not of concrete but of paper. The work of the Ontario Hydro and New York Power Authority consultants resulted in an agreed-upon estimate of the hypothetical amount of power there would have been with the raising of the dam. BC would provide an equivalent amount of power at a price equal to that which Seattle would have paid to raise the dam and over the same time period. The United States and Canada entered into a treaty to guarantee the performance of Seattle and BC over the life of the agreement. And while all of this seems relatively straightforward, the level of complexity of the negotiations and the number of cross-border institutions that had to sign-off on the final agreement and treaty was remarkable. They included the city of Seattle, the province of British Columbia and all of their respective agencies, ministries and departments, the U.S. State Department, the Federal Energy Regulatory Commission, the U.S. Department of Energy, the Interior Department, and, by virtue of the treaty, the United States Senate. It included the Canadian Department of External Affairs and all of the other Canadian federal entities that had any authority on any of the matters pertinent to the agreement and the treaty.

And through it all was Keith being Keith. When the agreement had been reached in principle, the commission was invited to brief the Seattle City Council. At one point a Council member by the name of Virginia asked why it was important to have a treaty in addition to the agreement. The answer, of course, was that Seattle had reached an agreement with BC before, only to see it evaporate as a result of a political change in BC. Keith, however, looked straight at Virginia and said "Virginia, I've had four wives, I've dined with Presidents, I own a world champion race horse, and I've elected senators and governors. But, Virginia, I've never had a treaty."

On April 2, 1984 Keith got his treaty. In an impressive treaty-signing ceremony at the U.S. State Department then Secretary of State George Schultz and his counterpart, the Canadian Minister of External Affairs, Paul McEachern, signed the treaty they described as the "Bulen-Olson Treaty."

When Keith first came to the commission, he told me that we would do good work together, important work, uplifting things, that he was a visionary and that we would have fun. Like so many people that have worked with Keith, I found myself asking that weary question—are we having fun yet? Well, I did have fun, and the number of times that Keith laughed at me, that I laughed at Keith, that we laughed at and with each other are too many to count. They are among the most cherished memories of my lifetime.

Will Rogers once said that he never met a man he didn't like. In *The New York Times* front page picture of Ronald Reagan giving his first term acceptance speech, the Reagan advance team had a big banner draped directly over the podium which read "Will Rogers never met Keith Bulen." This was true. Will Rogers never did meet Keith Bulen and that's a pity, because if he had he would have liked Keith, he would have liked him very much. So many people have now been called American originals that to use the phrase has become trite. In truth, Keith was not an American original but he was quintessentially American. And I can think of no better tribute to my friend. When the Reagan advance team hoisted that banner, the message was not meant to damn Keith Bulen, but rather to pay him tribute. It was a tribute that he richly deserved.

One person can still make a difference.

David LaRoche served as the Chairman of the New Hampshire Democratic Party, as the United States Secretary of the International Joint Commission, and is currently an independent environmental consultant.

New People

No cause is worth its weight in salt if a proponent can't convince others to join the ranks. That's as true in politics as it is in religious or charitable work. Bulen, and the candidates he promoted, brought hundreds, maybe thousands, of new people to politics, and you know how the old saying goes —if good people don't get involved, who will? Up until only weeks before his death, Keith was regularly meeting with young people and encouraging them to become involved in the two party political process. Coming up are comments by four good people—a young judge, a prosecutor, a highly successful businessman, and a community leader.

Up Front

by Cale Bradford

Keith was the first person to contribute to my campaign when I decided to seek judicial office and he was a mentor who is always ready to offer advice to young people entering public life. Keith was important in my life, so I have given some thought as to what I might want to say about Keith Bulen and it is a conversation I once had with my father that has always stuck in my mind.

I commented to my father how direct and to the point I observed Keith to be. My father replied, that "There are very few people in this world who you know where you're at right up front . . . and there's a helluva' lot to be said for that."

I couldn't agree with my dad more!

Cale Bradford is Judge of the Marion Superior Court, Criminal Division 3, in Indianapolis.

Coronation

by Scott C. Newman

"You can wear that at your coronation." Those, I believe, were Keith Bulen's first words to me, uttered after he approached and grabbed hold of the velvet hunt collar of my new Chesterfield coat. I have since been the victim of Keith's acerbic commentaries on dozens of humbling occasions. Humbling only in the sense of how much I had to learn; uplifting in that a man of the political and intellectual firepower of Keith Bulen would include my two campaigns for Marion County Prosecutor among his projects and passions.

Between thrusts of Keith's rapier wit and mouthfuls of Jonathan Byrd Cafeteria's mashed potatoes, I learned a great deal from the man. One could distill powerfully from the things he condemned, that which he held dear. When he condemned a candidate's absorption in matters of fundraising, he uplifted the need for the candidate to become more devoted to people. When he bemoaned television and news reporters, he reaffirmed that politics conducted properly must be about direct service and real, unfiltered relationships. When he grabbed hold of the lapel of your Chesterfield, you better begin to appreciate that the grass roots is everything, and all else is a paltry second-best.

The problem with it, of course, is that only a man with the superhuman drive, the zest, the passion for life, and the fertile mind of a Keith Bulen could look at a county of 840,000 people and be undaunted by the task of getting to know them all, and I mean really getting to know them. The rest of us hope we won't fail too miserably if we can accomplish about one-third of what he prescribed for us.

I described his capacities just now as "superhuman," but tragically we are all finding out that this isn't literally true. Conditions all too human finally attacked him. But whatever evil molecule first decided to become a turncoat to Keith's body, and to lead other molecules and treacherous cells to do the same, they fell only against the husk that surrounded a soul of enormous proportions, a soul that cannot be attacked by any cancer. It is a soul that has attained already a measure of immortality, as it has forever changed the landscape of our entire state, and as it forever commands us to know what we're about, to give every ounce of energy to our fellow men, to shake their hands, listen to their voices, come to their doorsteps, take the bold but well-considered gambles, smash the idols, remember the birthdays, treasure the friendships, savor the victories, laugh at life's knockdowns and by all means, save the high-and-mighty stuff for the coronation.

_____

Scott Newman is the twice elected Prosecuting Attorney for Marion County, Indiana

A Man of Many Talents

by John Burkhart

As you grow older and look back over the preceding years, you realize that many helpful things have come your way—that you have been the recipient of assistance that made possible results that you have long thought of as your own accomplishments. Many years ago, Keith Bulen came into my life. Not only did he serve as my personal mentor, he transformed our whole community through an organization that he envisioned and conceived. That organization and its accomplishments in Indianapolis and Indiana gained national attention.

Keith was a man of many talents, especially in the area of politics and government. Without the leadership of such gifted performers, the rest of us would often be baffled by what is needed next. Keith knew what to do next because he always had a well conceived game plan for every endeavor.

He made himself available for leadership at a time when county Republicans were going through an era of internal organizational fights, but he had the patience and skills to bring that civil war to an end. The result was a very powerful political organization, built on loyalty, respect, and principle, that was successful in placing many of its talented leaders in elected and appointed office at the local, state, national, and international levels.

As a person interested in the success of my community, my state, and my nation, I feel deeply indebted to Keith Bulen.

John Burkhart was a co-founder of The College Life Insurance Company of America. He also co-founded the Indianapolis Business Journal *along with papers in St. Louis, Pittsburgh, Philadelphia, Baltimore, Cincinnati, and Dallas. He served as Chairman of Bulen's Candidate Selection Committee.*

To Be The Best

by Anne Calvert Schuster

It has been one of my great privileges of life to work as a volunteer with L. Keith Bulen, whom I considered the consummate "Master In Politics." To work with Keith was to be stimulated, educated, and appreciated. Yes, sometimes it was frustrating because Keith was a perfectionist and meeting his demands was always a great challenge. He was demanding, but from responding to his demands, one was challenged to undertake difficult assignments and to be the "best." His expectations of his friends and coworkers were unlimited, but the rewards of having done one's best were great. An outstanding facet of Keith's character was his loyalty to those who shared his feelings and beliefs in good government. Not only did he reward those who shared his patriotic fervor, he gave of himself to provide them with unstinting support and appreciation.

On the flip side of Keith's demanding soul there existed a sensitive, caring, gentle, man. My husband's and my friendship of many years with Keith privileged us to see the inner Keith. We have seen his tears of compassion and have known of his many unsung and generally unknown supportive acts to his multitude of friends and acquaintances. We shared many conversations with him when he spoke of the pride he had in the young people who have taken up the mantel he laid down and who have been inspired to become politically involved by his teachings and his leadership. Some of these people can now be found all throughout our nation where they are carrying on his teachings.

I thank my husband for encouraging me to become associated with Keith as a volunteer in Republican political endeavors and governmental activities. It has been tremendously rewarding. Dwight and I have each gained invaluable knowledge, insight, and some expertise, through our association with the "master." We remain dedicated to do our part to promote the honest, efficient, intelligent, political policies taught by Keith and we are proud to be a part of the "Bulen team."

L. Keith Bulen was the epitome of a true American who was unashamed to display his patriotism. Through his drive and determinism he became a leader who put his patriotism into action through his belief that all people, all political parties, must work for the common good through the promotion of good government.

Annie Schuster and her husband Dr. Dwight Schuster are well known in the Indianapolis area. Annie, a high school English teacher, was a founder of WINS—Women In Neighborhood Service—which was a Bulen conceived idea to permit the Republican Party to show its heart to those in need. She has been a precinct committeeman and served as a Bulen volunteer for more than thirty years.

The Heart Of Grassroots Politics

by Gerry C. LaFollette

From my experiences as a journalist covering politics for more than forty years (and being interested in it all of my life), I discovered that there are two kinds of people involved - the back room organizer and the out front candidate. Keith Bulen was as superb in his role in the back room as was his prize out front candidate Richard Lugar as a two-term mayor of Indianapolis, four term (and counting) United States Senator, and Presidential candidate. Often overlooked is the fact that Keith himself had been a candidate and election winner as a State Representative. Perhaps that made him a better man behind the scenes because he understood candidates—he had been there, done that.

My first recollections of Keith on a full time basis was in the spring of 1966. He was going around Marion County attending the township Republican clubs, meeting the precinct committeemen in his campaign to defeat GOP County Chairman H. Dale Brown. The precincts are the heart of grass roots politics. How appropriate! For Keith, that's where the action always was because that is where a leader could build an organization.

Keith did just that and he won.

The next year he went out on a limb backing a young school board member for mayor —Dick Lugar. Alex Clark, who had been mayor in the early 1950s, also wanted the Republican nomination. An epic struggle took place, but it wasn't the only one. On the Democratic side an even more titanic battle took place with County Chairman James Beatty challenging his own incumbent mayor, John Barton. There's been nothing like it before or since. When the votes were counted, Barton and Lugar were the winners.

As soon as he could, Keith put out overtures to the Clark camp, so the party could close ranks for the fall. For Keith, once a primary was past, the Democrats were the foe. In 1967, Keith healed party wounds. The Democrats never did and Lugar was elected as mayor of Indianapolis. In some respects that was Keith's finest hour—for what it meant to Indianapolis, to Indiana, to the United States, and to the world. Winning Republican control of Indianapolis also helped Keith enter the ranks of the state GOP and the Republican National Committee.

Keith was successful in the Nixon campaigns and many others, but I consider 1980 as his second finest hour. He was in charge of the eastern United States in the 1980 presidential campaign of Ronald Reagan. His efforts can be verified if one looks at the vote totals of 1980 compared with Gerald Ford four years earlier. The margins of victory in traditionally difficult states for the GOP were not that wide. And, although many factors are important in close wins, there is no doubt that Keith made the difference in several states.

If Keith had any disappointments, one may have been not getting Lugar on the 1980 ticket as the Vice Presidential nominee with Reagan. At the start of the GOP convention in Detroit, many political pundits thought Lugar was the man—younger than Reagan, intelligent, and a man of integrity. But it was not to be. For Indiana and the nation, we can only ponder, "what if?"

Making a difference may as good a way as any of summing up Keith's role in the politics of Indianapolis, Indiana, and the nation. Keith made a difference.

At the same time, he was a teacher. The list of those who worked with and learned from Keith is impressive and influential:

Mitch Daniels—who ran Lugar's senate campaigns, headed the National Republican Senatorial committee, and served as political advisor to President Reagan.

Gordon Durnil—who ran both of Robert Orr's winning races for governor and served as Indiana Republican State Chairman during the Reagan/Orr years.

Mike McDaniel—managed lieutenant governor and gubernatorial campaigns for John Mutz and is Indiana Republican Chairman at this writing.

Bruce Melchert—former Indiana GOP Chairman and campaign manager and advisor for Mayor Bill Hudnut.

Mark Miles—managed Hudnut's 1979 re-election and managed the 1980 Dan Quayle upset over three-term incumbent U.S. Senator

Birch Bayh.

Dr. Dennis Nicholas—long-time Marion County Coroner, who chaired the Reagan Indiana campaigns in 1976, 1980, and 1984.

John Sweezy—Marion County GOP Chairman since Keith stepped down in 1972.

Mike Wells—who ran the 1978 campaign for prosecutor of an unknown attorney named Stephen Goldsmith, who later served two terms as the mayor of Indianapolis.

And there are many other young people who would not have entered public life were it not for the example set by Keith, as well as his personal encouragement and support for each.

As a journalist, I tended to believe the people with whom I dealt. I always thought that Keith answered my questions truthfully—but, I was fully aware that it was up to me to ask the right questions.

Gerry C. LaFollette was a reporter for The Indianapolis Times *from 1958 to 1965 when it folded. He then was a reporter for* The Indianapolis News *from 1965 to 1988, when he retired. He was selected as a Nieman Fellow at Harvard University.*

Managing Volunteers

by George W. Geib

Of all the organizational features that characterize the Marion County GOP, few are more significant than its management structure. All Indiana counties are made up of precincts, usually with between 500 and 1000 registered voters residing in them. Unlike most Indiana counties, however, where the number of precincts was small, Keith Bulen was chosen to head a county organization where precincts numbered in the hundreds. Because each was entitled to both a committeeman and a vice committeeman (one of each sex), it was a manifest impossibility to maintain ongoing personal contact with precinct leaders all throughout the county. Nobody had tried to do so in years. Instead, a band of powerful but little known middle managers, the ward chairmen, had provided that function. Grouped in thirty-two numbered wards in the pre-Unigov city, and in party administrative wards in the outlying townships, the ward leaders carried a varied portfolio of responsibilities that extended from committeeman recruitment to direction of voter contact programs.

Under Bulen's predecessor, H. Dale Brown, the ward leaders had been creatures of the chairman and his headquarters. Each ward chair was expected to provide supportive votes in party caucuses and conventions, as well as to deliver needed numbers on their wards precinct voting machines on both primary and general election days. Dale Brown's meetings with his ward leaders at the Columbia Club had often featured a person by person review of past and future performance that one observer called the "come to Jesus" school of politics.

Yet many ward leaders found themselves pulled by another loyalty to their committeemen. In both 1962 and 1964 the county had seen a series of primary and general election defeats under Dale Brown that caused many to question his autocratic style of operation. Soon a growing number of reform-minded precinct committeemen, who themselves had to stand for election in the primary every two years, started sending messages that they expected their ward leaders to transmit. In 1966 the issue came to a head over the question of ward chairman selection: should the position be appointed by the county chairmen, or elected by the committeemen? Bulen as chairman opted for the latter, but was known to bemoan the independence it encouraged in some wards and precincts.

If one wonders why the loyalty of precinct leaders was so important, it's well to remember that the GOP depended heavily upon those workers for the actual voter contact activities that could add the one or more vote per precinct that might determine success for the entire county. Precinct office would, if anything, increase in importance thanks to the state legislatures decision in 1965 to approve door-to-door voter registration and to permit the major parties to credential their volunteers for that purpose. A well motivated volunteer who would undertake such tasks, especially in the heat of August and early September, was a valuable contributor to victory.

Yet a traditional motivater of many GOP precinct workers, patronage, was not what it once had been. Partly the problem was specific to the Democrat Party surge of the mid-1960s, when national, state, city, and many county offices were in opposition hands and the rewards went to their workers and supporters. But partly the problem was the decline of patronage itself, much of it about to be swept away in the name of reform. Whether as cause or effect, a growing number of party workers began to appear who were motivated by personalities, ideas, and issues, and not by the expectation of government employment after election. The Goldwater candidacy of 1964 was extremely important in this shift, and its legacy continued to be felt throughout the coming years. Bulen was certainly able to use patronage when it became available to him, as both a fund raising and a recruiting tool. But viewed in retrospect, it's clear that he also recognized the new face of volunteerism.

Today there is an extensive literature on volunteerism, much of it generated in response to a perceived decline in total numbers of people with available time and willingness to work without pay. Much of that literature suggests that the task of the volunteer manager is to create a situation that reflects the workplace—with clear assignments, training, supervision, recognition, and the possibility of promotion. If so, Bulen's approach to volunteer activity would probably stand up well to contemporary inspection. Party schools, uncommon under his predecessor, became common—including well remembered Victory Colleges. Township and ward level meetings often incorporated motivational sections, frequently in the form of candidate presentations. Running a successful Marion County GOP operation has evolved considerably over the last quarter of a century, but the growing dependence upon volunteerism owed much to the management directions set in motion by Keith Bulen in his era.

George W. Geib is a Professor of History at Butler University in Indianapolis. He is also a long time volunteer at Marion County Republican Headquarters, and a highly talented trainer of precinct workers.

From The Hill

Can we believe what we hear from Washington?

When the following speak—the answer is YES!

Chanters

by Dan Burton, M.C.

I first met Keith Bulen when I was a fledgling politician. He and I were both members of the Murat Shrine Chanters. He was a baritone and believed himself to be a great singer (he wasn't bad, but you know Keith—always reaching higher).

I discovered, during our conversations at the Shrine, that Keith had been a State Representative, and that he was interested in becoming chairman of the Marion County Republican Party. I was a young ward chairman in the party, and he convinced me and many others that he had the leadership qualities necessary to change our party from a losing organization to a winner. He was so convincing that when the Republican Action Committee was formed to oppose the existing party organization, he convinced me to help start an organization called the Young Republicans For Action.

Keith was so inspiring that those of us who were active as young Republicans were called upon to spend an inordinate amount of time assisting the Republican Action Committee take control of the official party apparatus. Because of Bulen's leadership and determination, the Action Committee not only replaced the old leadership, but won a tremendous electoral victory in November of 1966, which started a string of successes that continues today—more than thirty years later.

Keith was a tremendous help to me personally, in addition to being the great political leaders he was for our party. Under his tutelage, I learned not only organizational politics, but some political strategies which ultimately led to my election to the Congress.

Keith Bulen was a hard driving leader. He demanded the best and was very tough at times, but he also showed real compassion and concern for his friends, both in and out of politics. He was a visionary who could see a little further down the political road than his contemporaries. Because of that he was an invaluable advisor to leaders at all levels of government–local, state and national.

Keith advised, governors, Congressmen, Senators, Presidents, and young people just getting started. All who know him respect and admire his abilities. Although Keith and I have had many differences through the years—some that were very strong, I considered him to be not only a good friend but my political mentor. His caring represents a large part of the reason why I have been able to succeed.

Dan Burton is a Member of Congress from the 6th District of Indiana.

Keith Was No Saint

by Andy Jacobs, Jr.

Keith Bulen was one of my favorite political people because he was good at it and because he was funny, one of the fastest wits in the (mid) West.

He played to win, but in the manner of the Germans and Allies in World War One, he always had time to sing a few verses of "Lili Marlene" with the opposition. Even in the thick of late October competition, he genuinely enjoyed sharing jokes about tactics with managers and candidates of the Democratic Party.

Keith liked to go first cabin. When he was single and dating a staffer in the "enemy" camp on Capitol Hill, her boss—dare I say Vance Hartke?—required her to work late enough to miss the last plane for Indianapolis, Keith and dinner, and, well . . .. She flew to Indianapolis that night anyway. The story was that Keith chartered a private jet and paid full fare for his lady fair.

The first time I saw Keith, he was a deputy prosecutor standing in a hallway of the old Marion County Court House. He was being verbally assailed by none less that the alleged gambler, Tuffy Mitchell. The amused look on Keith's face could not have been comforting to the little tough guy standing in front of him. I believe Keith said something like, "Don't give me any grief about this. I'm not involved." Keith sent him to someone else—anyone else.

Keith was no saint—few are— but he was a towering factor in the politics of Indianapolis and, to a significant extent, to the politics of North America including Canada. And for the most part, he helped make it fun.

Andy Jacobs, Jr. served 30 years as a Member of Congress from Indianapolis (11th and 10th Districts).

Best Game In Town

by William H. Hudnut, III

While Keith and I did not have much opportunity to work together officially, since he left as Marion County Chairman about the time I began my political career, I will always be grateful to him for two things. First, he got me started in politics, which, looking back, was probably the happiest and most satisfying part of my life. I would never have made it to first base in the screening process without his interest and support.

I won the 1972 primary for Congress by a scant 82 votes (it went up to 98 after the recount, out of a total of some 45,000, which is why I was called "Landslide Hudnut"), and know I would never have won that election, or the one in the Fall, without Keith's involvement.

I admired him a lot, ever since I first heard him give one of his stem-winders at a rally in the late 1960s, and felt that he represented the kind of vision, commitment, reformist zeal, and inspiration, that I wanted to be a part of. Then John Sweezy came in as county chair, and my official relationship with Keith ended. But I continued to seek him out on occasion for advice and insight, which he always offered. And this is reason number two —his mentoring friendship across the years. Here's but one example: I had an in-depth conversation with him before appointing the first African American deputy mayor in the history of the city, not to ask him whether or not I should do it, but to get his input on how. I gave him a key to the city somewhere along the line, as a token of my esteem.

I loved politics. It was the best game in town. Keith taught me how to play it, and while I do not fault him for my mistakes and shortcomings, I will always give him credit for the enthusiasm and commitment to public service which he instilled in me.

William H. Hudnut, III, a Presbyterian minister, was elected to Congress in 1972 and served four terms as Mayor of Indianapolis (1976-1991)

An Enduring Army

by Senator Richard G. Lugar

The Indianapolis School Board was conducting well attended and sometimes volatile hearings on voluntary racial integration in 1965 when I received a note from Keith Bulen indicating that he liked my style and encouraging my personal leadership. I did not know him then, but I heard a lot about him in 1966 as he and a band of veteran Marion County officeholders displaced Marion County Republican Chairman, H. Dale Brown.

In July of 1966, I had anticipated being elected as President of the School Board, but a 4-3 vote by a new majority effectively ended a search for voluntary racial integration and my leadership in that quest. I accepted the invitation of Paul R. Oakes to manage his Congressional campaign for the old 11th District. This was an energetic and idealistic struggle that was recognized as being remarkably competitive, though ultimately unsuccessful. But Chairman Bulen and the rest of the GOP county ticket swept to victory.

The county offices offered substantial patronage for the Marion County Republican organization. But the giant prize was mayor of Indianapolis, and in 1967, Democratic incumbent John J. Barton stood for reelection.

In January of 1967, I expressed a strong interest in the office, but in subsequent weeks former Republican Mayor Alex Clark and Judge William Sharp entered a pre-primary contest centered around a "slating committee" of 28 party officials. I was selected in early March to be the candidate. But Mayor Clark did not accept the verdict, nor did many organizational leaders who had never heard of me and found the slating committee result incredible.

The subsequent primary campaign would determine control of the party. Keith Bulen had the task of guiding a novice into big city politics. He gave me crash courses in fund-raising and handling the media, and he oriented me to a host of neighborhood and ethnic considerations that were much broader than those affecting school board debates. We survived the May primary test by a vote of roughly

21,000 to 17,000. The next challenge was the Democratic incumbent mayor, who was scandal free and presiding over an apparently prosperous city.

I had a vision of achieving excellence for Indianapolis and plans for expansion based on case studies of Nashville and Davidson County, Tennessee; and Jacksonville and Duval County, Florida. My confidence and trust in Keith grew strong as he accepted what I knew were exceptionally bold and controversial programs. His confidence and trust in me grew as he perceived, accurately, that I was both astonished at and appreciative of his political creativity and comprehensive grasp of detail. He was brutally frank in his advice, indefatigable in pushing himself and all around him to the limit, and a frequent shield for me from the underbelly of political combat.

Keith employed photographers and sound technicians of national reputation. One early Sunday morning, I walked back and forth across a downtown intersection more than seventy times while a photographer caught the perfect "walking man" shot. Keith reproduced the photo on a billboard, fifty feet wide, overlooking the old West Washington Street bridge. On the weekend before the November general election, Keith produced a biographical supplement inserted into *The Indianapolis Star*. This was the first information that thousands of voters had about me, but if was sufficiently convincing to generate substantial support.

Keith sent out tens of thousands of letters to registered voters that were returned to GOP headquarters indicating the possibility that a voter was no longer eligible to vote in a certain precinct. A battalion of young lawyers and professional persons were recruited to stand watch for twelve hours at each precinct in question. They challenged all voters suspected of illegal procedure. Despite these confrontations, which led to the arrest and removal of many of the GOP professional watchers, I learned in subsequent months from some political activists for the opposition that they had voted against me as many as seven times each.

Victory came by a vote of roughly 71,000 to 64,000. My wife, Char, and I drove to Hilton Head, South Carolina, for a week of rest. Within 72 hours, Keith arrived with a bulging brief case. He agreed to play golf just once, because we were playing, but he had come to do business. He had suggestions for virtually every executive and supervisory position in the city government. He proposed a patronage committee of veteran loyal party leaders to screen applicants for every job in which the mayor had any ability to hire or fire. The City-County Building was to be transformed from a Democratic Party stronghold to the crown jewel of Republican organizational strength, perhaps the strongest in the country.

I was surprised by Keith's comprehensive urgency, and he was equally surprised by the speed of my decisions and agreement with his personnel and organizational suggestions. We shared a determination to start a new government on January 1, 1968, that was not only prepared to answer the phones and provide prompt service, but that would be exciting for all citizens in Indianapolis and the 45 percent of Hoosiers in the Indianapolis television viewing area.

The promise of the campaign had been to create a new Indianapolis, a city of excellence in aspiration and greatness in achievement. Even if voters were not certain how and when all of this would happen, they had confidence that we had a vision and a plan. But candidates for urban leadership all over America often have had visions and plans. The indispensable factor that so frequently was missing was a political organization that could produce majority votes to enact the visions and plans.

Nineteen sixty-eight offered an unparalleled opportunity for Marion County Republicans to exert a major influence in the selection of a new governor of Indiana, a strong Republican legislature, and even a President of the United States. The political genius of Keith Bulen was equal to these challenges. The consolidation of Indianapolis and Marion County in the 1969 Indiana General Assembly with a strong elected mayor and a twenty-nine member council was based upon political election results and relationships forged in the Indiana and national GOP conventions of that year and the successful campaigns that followed.

With Keith's intervention usually paving the way, I was asked to introduce Richard Nixon in pre-primary rallies in Washington, Indiana, and Southport, and to give the keynote speech at the Indiana GOP Convention. I also was given the opportunities to serve as both a convention delegate and one of two Indiana members on the National GOP Platform Committee at Miami Beach, where I was introduced to a host of national political columnists and played golf with George Schultz.

This was all thirty years ago, but these events remained vivid in Keith Bulen's memory as they do in mine. He was to become GOP National Committeeman from Indiana and a major leader in the nomination and election of President Ronald Reagan. He served our nation with distinction in many domestic and foreign diplomatic roles. But when I saw Keith at a Marion County Republican meeting in February of 1998 surrounded by a remarkable number of "slating committee members" from 1968 and legislators who voted for and perfected Unigov in 1969, I knew that his successes and my own are based on the idealism and loyalty of successful politicians—persons who love people and who are prepared to visit, press the flesh, raise money, give speeches, and compete without rest until mountains are climbed.

Fortunately, Keith Bulen found and organized an enduring army of such people in Marion County, Indiana.

Richard G. Lugar is the Senior United States Senator from Indiana. He also served two terms as Mayor of Indianapolis.

The First Symposium

The inaugural Bulen Symposium On American Politics was held in front of two hundred or so interested members of academia, news media, and practicing politicians, on December 1, 1998. David Broder, of *The Washington Post*, keynoted the affair and wrote an excellent summary of the day long symposium:

Person To Person In Indiana
By David S. Broder
Wednesday, December 9, 1998

INDIANAPOLIS: It could have been a lugubrious occasion—a symposium on a feeble institution, the two-party system, honoring a political leader with an incurable illness. Instead, the first annual Bulen Symposium on the Indiana University-Purdue University campus here was as bracing as my end-of-the day visit with L. Keith Bulen, the storied GOP power broker to whom this day was dedicated.

As the longtime Marion County (Indianapolis) chairman and Indiana Republican National committeeman, Bulen helped launch and sustain the notable career of Sen. Dick Lugar and sponsored a succession of successful mayors and governors. He was a key national strategist for both Richard Nixon and Ronald Reagan. Throughout his career, Bulen demonstrated a talent for organization, a shrewd appreciation of human nature and an understanding that great changes (such as the creation of city-county regional government in this area) demand strong parties.

Parties like that are hard to find in these days of individualized campaigns built around TV messages. Most of the out-of-state scholars, operatives and political journalists who came to the day-long seminar at the invitation of Mitch Daniels, a former Reagan White House political director, cited evidence of ever-weaker parties at the national level and in their states.

Paul Allen Beck of Ohio State University said that the parties had no one to blame but themselves. As they have become more centralized and more professionalized, he said, "they have changed from labor-intensive to capital intensive structures." That is, they find it easier to raise money to buy TV-ads than to work on face-to-face contact with the voters. And that, of course, is one of the main reasons voter turnout continues to decline.

But Indiana is an exception—and perhaps, because of the Bulen legacy, a harbinger of better days ahead for both parties. Wabash College political scientist David J. Hadley, writing earlier this year in a publication of Indianapolis' Sycamore Institute, said Indiana elections are notable for pitting two well-organized, competitive parties against each other." Republicans have dominated at the presidential level, but Democrats have won the last three gubernatorial elections and match up well in Senate, House and legislative races.

Republican state Chairman Mike McDaniel, a Bulen protege, and Democratic state Chairman Joe Andrew explained how they do it. The testimony from Andrew, a lawyer who is currently under discussion for the vacant post of national Democratic chairman, was particularly impressive, because the state has many more Republican-inclined voters than Democrats.

In his four years in the job, he has recruited volunteer precinct chairmen for virtually every neighborhood and "empowered every one of our 4,800 chairmen as the campaign manager for his or her precinct." On computer printouts or CD-ROMs, they receive from state headquarters walking lists of the voters to see in their precincts, each identified by party inclination and issue interests, and a suggestion of talking points to use in urging them to vote. Andrew said he is convinced that with the splintering of the TV audience into cable channels and the skepticism about 30-second spots, "the personal message from a neighbor or a peer is the only thing that gets through to people."

It works. Last month, in addition to giving ex-governor Evan Bayh the biggest Senate victory margin ever achieved by an Indiana Democrat, his party broke a tie in the state house of representatives and gained a 53-47 majority. Andrew told me, "There's a direct line from what Keith Bulen did in his time to what I'm trying to do now. We're just doing the old-fashioned things with new tools."

Bulen was too weakened by cancer to attend the symposium, but when I drove out to his house, I found him as engaged in the politics of the day as ever. As his life comes to an end, he knows that his legacy remains in the strong parties of his home state—an example to the nation.

Two great Democrats died last week. Former senator Albert Gore Sr., the vice president's father, was a man of enormous charm and limitless courage, who stood up for his beliefs and opposed segregation and the war in Vietnam when many of his constituents were not willing to let go of either one. It cost him his seat in 1970, but it solidified an enduring reputation for principled political leadership. The other was Matthew Reese, a genial giant who helped win the crucial 1960 primary in his home state of West Virginia for John F. Kennedy and then taught a generation of Democrats and liberal organization leaders how to make their case to the voters. Matt never forgot that politics is all about people. He, too, will be missed.

Next in the proceedings, the chairs of the two national political parties, Governor Roy Romer, Democrat, and Republican Jim Nicholson, made presentations under the watchful wit of emcee Mark Shields, and the chairs of the Indiana Republican (Mike McDaniel) and Democratic (Joe Andrew) committees expressed their views as expert panels discussed "America's Political Parties: From the Machine Age to Virtual Reality?"—"We're Still Giving Elections–Is Anyone Coming?"—"Revitalizing Parties: Omens & Portents."—"Jesse 'The Body' Politic: What Will it Take to Reinvigorate the Electorate?" The complete faculty for the first symposium are listed in the appendix.

Sheila Suess Kennedy, an organizer of the first symposium, wrote her reflections in the December 30, 1998 issue of *The Indianapolis Star*.

E Pluribus Unum
By Sheila Suess Kennedy

On December 2d, IUPUI hosted the first annual Bulen Symposium. It was a remarkable gathering of nationally recognized scholars, journalists and practitioners of the political arts. The purpose of the daylong conference was to examine the health of America's two major political parties, but one could be forgiven for wondering whether the exercise wasn't akin to visiting a terminally ill patient to inquire about his acne.

Throughout the day, speakers shared insights about the contemporary political landscape. David Broder bemoaned the shift of power from parties to interest groups, with their narrower, more self-interested focus. Others pointed to trends undermining our form of government. The use of initiatives and propositions, for example, is hailed by many as "more democratic." But ours is not a democratic system; it is a representative democracy—a crucial difference.

Some speakers addressed the obvious—that television has reduced the importance of party activities like registration and polling. Others suggested that suburbanization has negatively affected the parties' grass roots. Suburban dwellers no longer know their neighbors, whose endorsement of a candidate or party no longer matters. Large lots make door-to-door efforts more difficult, and the sense of isolation so characteristic of suburban areas (neighborhood somehow doesn't seem the right adjective) erodes the sense of community upon which the political enterprise must ultimately rest.

If there was a recurring theme, it was the loss of connectedness, the fact that Americans no longer engage in a national conversation. As Samuel Freedman of The New York Times observed, we are seeing the "niching" of America, our division into a variety of market, ethnic and socioeconomic categories and subcategories. Sophisticated technologies allow political campaigns to send different messages to those in different "niches," just as the retail and service industries do. We have atomized our polity and truncated the American motto; we have lots of pluribus but not much unum.

As we enter the last year of the twentieth century, we desperately need agreement on a common enterprise, a communal vision that reminds us that we are all citizens and that our political institutions matter. Because it is the end of the century, it cannot be a vision that ignores where we are and where we have been; we cannot—attractive as the notion may seem to some—roll back the clock to a time of enforced homogeneity. We need to enter the 21st century with a shared mission that respects and honors our individuality, but insists that our differences be used creatively to define and advance the common good.

E Pluribus Unum does not require that we give up who we are in exchange for a place at the American table. It does require that each of us bring our different gifts and talents to that table, to sustain and nourish the American community.

Sheila Kennedy is a former Congressional candidate, former corporation counsel for the city of Indianapolis, and an assistant professor of law and public policy at the Indiana University School of Public and Environmental Affairs.

An evening dinner "In Tribute To Keith Bulen" was an emotional, but fun affair. Ken Bode, of *Washington Week In Review* on PBS, served as master of ceremonies. Senator Lawrence Borst, former Democrat State Chair Gordon St. Angelo, Margaret Hill-Chatham, former GOP National Committeewoman, and Rex Early, former GOP State Chair, gave tribute. Larry S. Landis, a soldier of the Bulen Era, presented the invocation:

Let us pray . . .

Here we are, Lord. For those of us who have participated in the Bulen Symposium today, this has been a pleasant day as we have shared our thoughts and insights, renewed old acquaintances, recalled old battles, some of them with each other, and engaged in spirited discussion.

For all of us, it is also an opportunity to honor and celebrate our friendship with Keith Bulen, to reflect on the ways in which he has touched our lives. And to ask that you hold him securely in the palm of your hand.

In quiet moments such as this, when we reflect on our individual and our collective efforts to make a difference in an imperfect world, we realize that even working together, we will inevitably fall short. And so, we need to recall that, in Lincoln's words, our concern should not be that you are on our side, but that we are on yours.

Bless this food. Bless this gathering. Bless the stories we will tell. Bless our laughter. Help us also to remember that even in the toughest of times, you are with us. And remind us that you are not through with us just yet, that we are works in progress, and we have more to do.

And when you call us to our next challenge, as you did your servant Isaiah, give us strength . . . give us wisdom . . . give us courage . . . give us humility . . . that we may respond with Isaiah . . . Here I am, Lord.

Amen.

From Fact To Fiction

by Gordon K. Durnil

I have successfully published two books of nonfiction and have now completed a novel. I find the writing of fiction to be much more difficult than nonfiction, because developing credible characters is so difficult. That's why fictional characters are usually based on real life people. If you knew L. Keith Bulen, you won't need to guess who was the pattern for the fictional character Larry Julian in my novel:

Pete's political mentor had pretty well retired from the political wars about ten years ago, but he was still somewhat involved. Prospective candidates regularly gave him the courtesy of stopping by once in a while seeking advice or his endorsement, but he didn't give his political activity the effort of old.

When in his prime, Larry Julian had been the absolute best.

The 1960s had been a time a great political upheaval. The civil rights movements, pro and con, were at the height of their public remonstrations. Streets were filled with young people who were protesting war, governmental malfeasance, and corporate greed. One generation thought the other had lost its way. The protesters wore funny clothes, had funny hair, but the ideas they promoted were not so funny. In the midst of that uproarious civic turmoil, Larry Julian ran a perfect campaign and elected a Republican as the mayor of the Democrat city. He did what the pundits said he could not do, and he did it with little money but with thousands of volunteers.

No one could organize a campaign, or a political party, better than Lawrence Julian. In his heyday, Larry Julian rebuilt the state party and turned it into a winner. From an absence of candidates, the party found itself well stocked under Larry's leadership. But now, aside from the quarterly lunches with his successful, but retired, volunteer army from three decades ago, Larry didn't do much in politics.

Pete called to ask Larry for a luncheon date because he needed advice from a friendly expert on how to handle the deals with Ralph Lee. Pete knew Larry would be opposed to a non-player buying his way to the front of the political line, but Pete wanted to hear the reasoning of the man in politics he most respected.

Larry Julian wasn't perfect. His ego was unrestrained, but he knew what candidates needed to do to get elected and he knew the relevance of why candidates did what they did. He knew how to build a loyal volunteer base and he could draft a campaign plan tailor-made for any candidate. He was a strong leader who could get people to willingly follow him. He was loyal to his beliefs and loyal to his followers, but Larry liked to take credit for successes whether he had anything to do with them or not. Sometimes he was publicly chastised for something he had nothing to do with, but had taken credit for, that later turned sour. The news media loved those situations.

Larry treated Bill Mooney as he would a friend, but more than once Moon reciprocated by ripping into Larry Julian's character on the front page of *The Comet/News*. Larry knew it was not possible to be friends with a reporter—reporters have no scruples—still Larry tried. He wanted everyone to be his friend. It was only after he was out of power that Larry learned too many of his many friends were of the fair weather variety.

As he was driving down to the south side of town, past his old grade school, on the way to Larry Julian's favorite lunch place, Pete relived many happy memories of the years he worked under Larry's leadership, winning election after election. Now Larry was his friend and confident.

The two were not always compatible. Larry did his best work at night, while Pete's best work was more likely to occur early in the morning before the phone starting ringing. All told, their teamwork had resulted in twenty years of one victory after another—the longest run of Republican victories in the history of the state.

The greeting between the two old war horses was warm, then the mentor led the pupil through the food line. Larry knew everyone behind the cafeteria line and challenged each one in a friendly banter. The owner came out front to welcome his friend and customer and Larry introduced Pete to most of the dining public, as well as to the employees. It took awhile to get seated, and even then several jokes had to be told, old stories remembered, as they ate their pie slowly to make it last longer.

Finally Larry asked, "What's wrong?"

Pete explained about the Nashville incident and went into great detail about the wants and desires of Ralph Lee.

"Save your marriage," was Larry's first advice. "Stay away from the girl." Larry had been married three times, but was spending his senior years alone.

"Let's you and I meet with the mayor and tell him that under no circumstances should Ralph Lee get the sewer contract. The mayor will be one of the first to go to jail if Ralph gets the deal, so let's make sure the mayor knows that."

Larry was decisive. He cared about Pete and he was not only giving his best advice, he was enlisting in the effort on Pete's behalf.

"Now," Larry continued, "let's find someone for the Senate seat that we can all get behind. Remember, we can't beat somebody with nobody. We need a body—a good candidate—someone who can overcome all of the Lee money. Where's Orvas and Quint in all of this? We need to get them on our side."

They sat at the booth for more than two hours after consuming their food. Pete's chicken pot pie was as good as any he'd ever tasted and the butterscotch pie was out of this world. When Pete left the cafeteria, he not only had the beginnings of a plan scratched on the back of a envelope, he had a strong ally—a friend.

Meeting with Larry Julian had been a good idea.

In real life, if you had a campaign to win, meeting with Keith Bulen was always a good idea.

What Can Only One Person Do?

Campaign Tips

To Asist Average Folks Seek Public Office

What Can Only One Person Do?

by a Bulen Protegé

People say that they are fed up with government. Some politicians have weak morals, some have weak "mentals," some have weak mettle, or so we hear. Do you agree? If so, what are you going to do about it?

If you really care, and if you are determined that change in government should take place, then why not run against that guy who keeps voting the wrong way?

Why not? It's your responsibility.

"Okay," you say. "I'll do it, I'll run for public office, but what do I do first?"

Good question. The first thing you do is find out if it's a constitutional office, such as legislator, or is it an office created by statute? Go to the public library and read what the constitution and the statutes have to say about the office. What are the qualifications to run? What are the filing dates and what are the requirements to file? Where do you file? What are the responsibilities and duties of the office? The answers to all of those questions can be found at a public library.

Once you are sure that you meet the qualifications to run, understand the basic duties of the office, and know when, where and how to file, you go to the next step.

The first thing you do is talk to your family, then your best friends, and the people you work with. Ask them what they think about you running for public office. Ask them in a direct and clear voice if they will support you. Don't say, "I hope you'll support me," and read yes in their eyes. Clearly ask, "Will you support me? Can I count on you to volunteer?" Hear them say yes, as most will. Seal the deal with a handshake.

Have a meeting with all the folks who say yes and come up with a name of someone who has held the office before, or someone who is involved in your political party structure. Visit that person and ask for advice. Don't leave that person without specifically asking for support. Your circle of family, friends and colleagues who support you, should be out asking their other friends, family, and associates, to also support you. The more people who sign on to your campaign, the better.

Name a campaign manager. Trying to manage your own campaign is a pretty good indicator that you have a fool for a candidate, because it's difficult to be objective about yourself. Important characteristics for a campaign manager are an organized mind, a willingness to work hard and long, and one hundred percent loyalty to you. Everything else can be learned. The ideal situation would be to attract someone with campaign experience to be your manager, as long as he or she possesses the above attributes.

Next, you determine the geographical boundaries of your election district. Then you and your campaign manager should spend hours driving the streets and alleys of the district. It's called windshield research. What kind of people live where? What are their problems?

As you have read, a 1967 mayoral campaign in Indianapolis did just that and found corners that needed stop signs, crumbling curbs, etc. Volunteers sent hand written letters wherein the candidate promised to fix those neighborhood problems. The candidate won the election and kept his word. But thirty years later, candidates for the State Senate in northern Indiana did not know the boundaries of their district. When the candidates were not listed on the ballot in three precincts a great hullabaloo erupted, all of which could have been prevented if the candidates had just taken time to learn the boundaries of the district.

The next step is to write a campaign plan. The purpose of the plan is to set out those things you need to do to win. Paid advertising, direct mail, yard signs, and materials to pass out as you go door-to-door talking with voters, are all expensive parts of the campaign.

Will you challenge the incumbent to a debate,—when, where and how many? What is the overall theme of your campaign? What colors and what slogan will you use on all advertising materials for consistency? What can you say or do to get your name in the news and raise your name awareness among the voters? All of those things and more should be in your campaign plan, which can be short and sweet or long and elaborate.

Once you've laid out an organized series of activities needed to win, write them down. If your campaign plan is not in writing, you don't have one. Next you cost out each necessity in the plan and create a budget. Now you know how much money you'll need to win. If the budget adds up to more than you think you can raise, rewrite the plan. Remember the plan comes first. The budget follows the plan.

Where's the money to fund your budget going to come from? You need a fund-raising plan, not a finance plan, but a fund-raising plan. What's the difference? Well a finance plan can get your fund raising volunteers thinking they might also have a role in determining how the funds are to be spent, something you've already figured out in your campaign plan. If it's a fund-raising plan, the focus is more narrow, dealing with a systematic method of obtaining the needed dollars.

Get a group of your supporters to help you raise funds, such as family, friends, and colleagues. Bankers aren't accustomed to asking for money, but salesmen are. Attorneys normally aren't very good at closing a solicitation, but realtors are. Physicians are too busy in their own world, but you can usually find a good person to solicit physicians. Set quotas for your fund-raisers, use peer pressure, reward their successes with recognition, and spend your money wisely.

There's an old story, famous among successful fund-raisers, about an indian chieftain out near the Rocky Mountains. He had killed more bears than any other known warrior. A newspaper man from the east drifted by one day, looking for the famous killer of bears. When he found him, he asked, "What's your technique? What strategy do you use that is so superior to other bear killers? What is the best way to kill a bear?" The old warrior was wise. He'd learned many things in his years as a warrior. He answered the question by saying, "The best way to kill a bear, is to just kill a bear."

The same is true in political fund-raising. The best way to get a contribution is to pick up the telephone or knock on the door and ask for it.

Okay, now you have some money in the bank. But what do you stand for? What's your vision? Why should contributors support you?

Why should voters vote for you? If you don't know the answers to those questions, you should end your campaign.

What three issues do you wish to stress in your campaign? Being upset about those issues isn't enough. You need to study them, understand them, refine your solutions, and then determine how to communicate those concepts to a public not always attuned to the ideas of candidates. Why not five, six or seven issues to discuss during your campaign? It's too many, that's why. Most voters will only hear your message a relative few times. If it's always different, you'll confuse the voters. So limit your messages and learn how to communicate them to the best of your advantage.

The following is a little more detail about two extremely important aspects of a political campaign—communicating your message and campaign research.

COMMUNICATING YOUR MESSAGE

Political advertising and public relations should accomplish four goals:

1. Acquaint voters with the candidate,

2. Create a positive perception about the candidate,

3. Build a pathway by which you can deliver the campaign message to the most people for the smallest per capita expenditure.

4. Motivate voters to vote for you in the sanctity of the voting booth, without assistance, over a sixty-second time frame, on one specific date.

MARKETING A CANDIDATE

Traditionally, political candidates have placed reliance on "earned media" to communicate their message to voters. Prior to television, such earned media forums were provided by newspapers, radio, public meetings and rallies. Television changed all of that. But change, as always, is a constant. As we near the end of the twentieth century, it's become very difficult to communicate a campaign message directly to voters. People no longer find their way, in appreciable numbers, to hear speeches by candidates. Political stories in newspapers are read by very few. Radio news has become very abbreviated. And now, with multiple channel choices, a large number of television watchers seldom watch television news. Talk radio and the internet have provided alternative channels for millions in limited targeted audiences.

A core group of primary election voters may be more observant of news reports than voters as a whole, but even they are not often very attentive. Marketing a contemporary candidate, therefore, requires innovative thought about how we get the candidate's message to the voter. Marketing a human candidate is profoundly different from marketing an inanimate product or service. That's why campaign hopes of hiring a "local" or "in state" advertising agency are often scrapped midstream in a political campaign and why campaigns who use advisors not expert in campaign advertising are so often losers.

Marketing a product or service provides the buyer with many opportunities to act. If she forgets to buy Acme Aspirin today, she can buy it tomorrow. When she walks by the place where her decision is to be made, brightly colored packaging helps her recall the advertising and prods her memory as she makes her decision. If a prospective buyer doesn't sign a contract to buy a new car today, the salesman can come back tomorrow, continuing to promote the car until the last moment when the decision is made and the contract is signed.

Political marketing, on the other hand, requires an expertise that will get the voter to the voting place to pull down one small poorly marked lever, or punch one confusing little shad out of a card, over a sixty second time frame, in a specific year, in a specific month, on one specific day, ONLY! If the decision desired by the marketer does not take place then, it is forever too late. The marketing campaign failed. The election lost. There's no packaging to recall the candidate's name in the voting place, because that's illegal. There's no one available to market the voter up to the time when the decision is made. That is also illegal. When decision time comes, the voter is alone with no reminders, constrained by time, and intimidated by voting machinery.

Marketing a human requires a building block process. The voter must get to know and like the candidate before the candidate's pronouncements on issues will be heard. You need not like an inanimate object such as an aspirin to make the decision to purchase it. But a voter does feel a need to have a positive feeling about the persona of a candidate in order to cast a ballot for that individual (especially true for top of the ticket candidates). President Clintn held support from the people for a long time partially because he was

ikable."

The goal of standard business advertising is to position the product or service in such a way as to garner a share of the market. Often, in business, a three percent or five percent share of the market can bring great financial rewards. In political advertising, anything less that a fifty percent market share makes you a loser. There is no rewarding second place in campaigns—you win or you lose. Obviously, some marketing principles hold true in any type of marketing, but the marketing of a political candidate does demand some very fundamentally different principles than required when marketing a product or service.

TELEVISION

Television is still overwhelming in its ability to reach voters with a campaign message, and television is usually the least expensive per capita method of doing so. No other medium comes close to competing with the impact television has as a delivery system for communicating candidate messages. Television makes the candidate a superstar. It helps with fund-raising. It is essential for a successful major campaign. Significantly more people will make their voting decisions from television commercials than from any other information source.

Sixty percent, or more, of a total major campaign budget should be dedicated to television advertising, because no other aspect of the campaign is as important. A competent and talented television consultant is essential in a statewide campaign to plan, shoot, edit, and produce winning television commercials. An experienced and fully equipped buyer of television time is essential to achieve the best placement at the lowest cost. In smaller campaigns, friends in the advertising or public relations business can volunteer to help with television advertising, but always remember, you get what you pay for.

We often hear public complaints about the high cost of campaigning, but, from the candidate's point of view, there is never enough money. So it's important to get the most bang for the buck. Television does that, but what can be a real shame is when candidates spend huge sums of money to put on bad spots—a not infrequent occurrence.

CABLE TELEVISION

Buying television ads via cable companies might be a good technique in a campaign, but advice from a knowledgeable practitioner of local television buys should be sought prior to any decision. Such networks as CNN, MSNBC, Fox News, ESPN, and other cable outlets are less than adequate substitutes for network television, but cable does give a candidate the opportunity to target news junkies, geographical areas, and other specialized groups.

RADIO

Radio can serve as a back up medium for television, as a substitute for television, or as a preferred medium for delivering specific messages. It's easier to target voters by radio, than by television, and there are some geographical areas covered only by out of state television where radio becomes a necessary vehicle. Conservative talk radio is especially good for Republican candidates in primary election contests.

NEWSPAPER

Most studies indicate that newspaper advertising for statewide political office is not an effective tool, but a special message for a specific community can be an effective rifle shot communication via newspaper. In smaller campaigns, the local newspaper may be the best source of information and advertising would be warranted.

BILLBOARDS

The major campaign value of billboards is name recognition, not perception building, although there have been cases where perception building by billboard has worked. Billboards may have some benefit in areas where out of state television dominates. But from a statewide perspective, a large scale billboard campaign can be nearly as expensive as a television campaign, without the broader benefits.

MAIL

Mail has been an effective tool in political campaigns, working very well as a backup medium for television and radio commercials. Normally, the most effective mail packages are self mailers with pictures and descriptions of the candidate, the candidate's background, the candidate's stand on the issues, and the candidate's vision. These mailers need not be high quality or expensive pieces. The tabloid format works very well. Mail is also valuable in a targeted fashion to tell voters reasons why they should not vote for your opponent.

TELEPHONE

We all hate to get telephone solicitations as we are eating dinner or watching our favorite television program, but there is evidence that advocacy phoning still works. It works especially well when tailored to fit the times—a message about the candidate on voice mail must be heard before the voter can hear the next message when working families come home to a house that has been empty all day. Telephoning, like mail, can be used for targeted messages suggesting why to vote for you or why to vote against your opponent. It also works well when it is coordinated with mail and other advertising.

FROM YOUR MOUTH TO THEIR EARS

The most effective way a candidate can communicate to voters is one-on-one. To do that the candidate must go where they are, so it is important to visit bowling alleys, schools, picnics, community events, and other gathering places. The best place to have a one-on-one discussion is at the voters home, so precinct walking and door knocking become essential elements of every campaign.

NEWSLETTER

A campaign newsletter is a good tool for communicating with campaign and party people, such as financial contributors, delegates to a state convention, volunteers, etc. It's a convenient forum to tell people reasons why they should support your campaign and work for your election. A campaign should build a mailing list, and continually add to it. The news media should be included on the newsletter list. Reporters will quite often give more credibility to information in a newsletter, than they will if the same information comes to them in a news release. Newsletters for specialized groups can be developed, such as the physicians, realtors, farmers, etc.

FAX AND E-MAIL NETWORKS

Extensive fax telephone number and e-mail address files should be developed in order to have instantaneous communications with supporters, party leaders, contributors, prospects, reporters, etc.

BROCHURE

A brochure, even if it's nothing more than a crutch for the candidate or for volunteer fund-raisers, is a necessary tool in most campaigns. Sometimes it's easier for a candidate to approach a prospective giver or voter, if the candidate has something to hand to the prospect. The brochure should be professionally done, but as inexpensively as possible. It's a one-on-one campaign tool used most often to tell people who you are, what you have done, what you will do for them in the future, and why they should vote for you.

CAMPAIGN BUTTONS AND BUMPER STRIPS

Campaign paraphernalia such as buttons and bumper strips do not make votes. They do help to keep your most avid supporters avid, because party activists often think a campaign without buttons is not a serious campaign. That makes the purchase of some buttons worthwhile, but don't buy more than will be used. Scarce buttons sometimes have more impact than those that are plentiful. Bumper strips should not be purchased in quantity if you don't have a realistic plan to get each strip on the bumper or window of a car.

NEWS CONFERENCES AND EARNED MEDIA

The candidate should meet with the news media as often as possible. To do so, it's important for the candidate to have a specific message. Most any activity warrants a news conference. Campaign leaders shouldn't be the ones to decide that too many news conferences are being held by the candidate. They should leave that decision up to the reporters. Hold news conferences as often as possible. A regular function of scheduling should have the candidate dropping in (usually prearranged) to meet with local radio station personnel, local newspaper reporters and editorial boards of local newspapers. Events should be planned that will attract the local news media to the event.

NEWS RELEASES AND ELECTRONIC ACTUALITIES

News releases should be drafted and distributed for most any occasion. Again don't worry about giving reporters too much paper. It's up to them to decide whether or not they'll use it. Radio actualities from speeches (taped in advance) can be good tools for getting the candidate's message on radio. Many smaller stations will use them regularly. Video-taped candidate statements can also be effective, but the television news folks are more reluctant to use them than are their colleagues in radio. Message delivery via satellite pickup by the television stations, or closed circuit television should also be investigated.

SPEECHES

The campaign issues should be restricted to three or four, but candidate speeches can be written so there is always fresh meat within the same old subject. That new meat should be highlighted and sent to the media as a part of a news release. The candidate's speeches should be critiqued from time to time by the campaign committee. Practice makes perfect and candidates need to continually practice their speechmaking. Candidates who give goofy speeches are normally not too attractive to voters. Candidates who don't understand what they're saying in a speech, written by someone else, are in big trouble.

POSTERS

Large posters with a picture of the candidate, his/her name, and the office sought should be prepared to appear in every voting place in the primary and general elections. Additional posters should be available for party booths at county fairs, political and community events, etc.

YARD SIGNS

Yard sign projects should be considered in some communities where the practice is expected and yard signs may be a good primary election tactic in targeted areas. Yard signs are worth some discussion, but normally not practical from a state wide volunteer distribution or monetary perspective. Yard signs are like kicking up dust, they indicate activity.

CANDIDATE INTRODUCTION

An introduction should be written for the candidate, to be carried at all times by the candidate and the candidate's driver or advance person. It can be handed to any person who is to introduce the candidate. The introduction should be brief and contain pertinent facts about the candidate, as well as other positive statements. A pre-prepared introduction is better for the campaign and will be appreciated by the master of ceremonies who comes to the microphone nervous and capable of saying anything.

PERSONAL COMMUNICATIONS FROM THE CANDIDATE

Letters to party leaders, notes to individuals met along the campaign trail, congratulations for accomplishments, etc., are all opportunities for "personal" notes or messages to be sent from the candidate. The "personal" notes can be the result of a computer program or originals from the candidate or staff advance person. Personal communications can be an effective tool in financial support and vote solicitation.

COMPUTER NETWORKING

Computer-and-internet-literate volunteers should be assigned the tasks of developing an e-mail network and/or a web site for communication purposes. Volunteers should be assigned the duty of frequently placing favorable candidate messages on various bulletin boards and chat forums. The numbers of Americans using e-mail and the internet is expanding at a rapid rate, with approximately one half of households on line at this writing.

CHRISTMAS CARDS

Will there be a massive Christmas card mailing from the candidate? If so, that decision needs to be made by Labor Day, with volunteers assigned to list development, card and envelope design, envelope addressing, etc. The initial reaction of many people to a massive Christmas card mailing by a political candidate is repugnance. The reaction of most of those who receive the cards is that it's a positive "personal" communication to them from the candidate. A Christmas mailing should be made to the basic political and community "mover and shakers," and to classmates from all schools you have attended, members of your social club, bowling team, union, etc. The mailing need not be a formal Christmas card. It could be a letter or some other creative piece. It is a time when people tend to open and read their mail.

POSTAL CARDS

Preprinted post cards with a picture of candidate, his or her name, office sought, and slogan, can be addressed and a short thank you note written on the way home from an event where the addressee was met by the candidate. A stamp can be affixed and dropped in the mail box on the way home, with the individual receiving a message from the candidate within a day or two following the meeting. It is an effective tool for impressing a prospective voter.

POLITICAL DINNERS

What advertising will you use at political dinners and how will you distribute it? Brochures, posters, photos of you and your family, are all common and are usually swept off the floor by the janitor after the meeting. Something a little unusual might be more effective, such as a place mat with your name, office and slogan. The place mat is more apt to remain in front of the diner than are brochures and other gimmicks.

PARAPHERNALIA

Items such as T-shirts, fingernail files, key rings, other gimmicks, etc., should be kept to an absolute minimum. None is normally enough. Occasionally, such items can be justified in association with a fund raising event or rally, but normally the consensus would be that funds spent on campaign paraphernalia are wasted funds.

CAMPAIGN RESEARCH

Winning campaigns need good information from which campaign decisions can be made. The gathering of such information is called campaign research. Campaign research need not be complicated, but it should be thorough, and it needs to commence at the very beginning of the campaign. The research can begin with a volunteer or a volunteer committee, but, in a major campaign, the research should very quickly become the responsibility of one person. The person in charge should build a volunteer committee (an opportunities committee) of experts in various fields, and should increase the size of the committee as the need for various areas of expertise are uncovered. Gathering research is just the first step. All such research must be put into a usable format, so the information is easily accessible to the candidate and is in a usable form for campaign needs.

SURVEY RESEARCH

The best survey research is the expensive, professional public opinion survey. Often samples of four hundred or six hundred people will meet the needs of the campaign, but optimum reliance can be put on a statewide survey with a random sample of eight hundred voters. It's from survey research that we find out what's on the minds of the voters, and what issues will move votes, so we know which issues to research further. The issues around which speeches and advertising are created are most reliably found in survey research.

Candidates who don't employ survey research will often talk about issues in which voters have no interest, or speak to issues about which voters are skeptical. When that happens, voters often do not "hear" what the candidate is saying, do not believe what he is saying or, don't care what he's saying, and the candidate loses the election.

Benchmark Survey. A benchmark survey is the early, large sample, comprehensive survey against which all future surveys are measured. The benchmark survey gives the campaign a good idea about the beginning basics of the campaign, such as name awareness and perceptions of the candidate and potential opponents. It highlights the issues which are foremost on the minds of voters as the campaign begins. The benchmark sets out various likely/less-likely push questions, warmness/coldness thermometer questions, the ballot test, etc. All information is broken out geographically and demographically.

Follow-up Surveys. Follow-up surveys are taken periodically to measure campaign progress. The follow-up questionnaires need not be as comprehensive as in the benchmark, because their purpose is to keep the campaign alert to potential voter shifts on issues, voter perceptions of the candidates, and the horse race ballot tests. Major campaigns should conduct a follow-up survey after waves of television advertising to measure the effectiveness of the advertising. Surveys are tools used to measure progress, so there is no need to take a poll if there has been no advertising activity, or scandal, since the last survey.

Tracking Surveys. Tracking surveys are a limited set of nightly telephone questions to a sample of one hundred fifty or so. The questions are usually ballot tests, issue tests and advertising tests. The purpose is to measure advertising success and to detect favorable or unfavorable trends. Tracking is most effective beginning two or three weeks before the election and ending four or so days prior to the election. Once a campaign can no longer place advertising, tracking becomes less of a campaign tool and more an item of personal interest. Tracking is to be looked at in sample batches of four hundred or more, which means a campaign should not form judgments until the first three days are in. Normally, that rule is violated. Decisions often are made on tracking samples too small for confident decision making. Tracking is meant for races which are extremely close, in the hope of detecting information over the final two weeks that can give the campaign an advantage.

ISSUE RESEARCH

Issue research should concentrate on major issues as identified from survey research and candidate interests. The issue committee (or staff person) should concentrate on the full development of at least four issues. A couple of likely "non-issues" should also be added to the mix (from either an offensive or defensive perspective), because non-issues often become issues of importance in campaigns. While issues that provide a contrast with an opponent are important, the campaign should also look for issues with which the opponent cannot disagree. By doing so, the campaign sets the agenda and assumes the mantle of leadership.

A common pitfall for many campaigns is to get bogged down in the research on thirty or forty issues. Ten may be a good number, four may be better. The number of issues to be researched should be determined by the candidate and campaign leadership, not by volunteer committees. Those issues should be prioritized in a clear enough fashion to guide the researchers work. Two or three (maybe four) issues will be the primary focus of a successful campaign, and by the time the general election arrives, issues of concern by the electorate have normally narrowed to one or two. The campaign, if it does its work well, can be responsible for determining what will be the decisive campaign issues on the voter's minds.

At the very least, the campaign should be prepared for a debate on the definitive issues. The way to do that is to be prepared for three or four issues, one of which will be the issue of the election. Issues of decisive significance often surface late in the campaign.

Consistency of issue discussion in speeches and advertising is critical for the duration of the campaign, which means the candidate says the same thing over and over. Many people will only have the opportunity to hear the candidate one time, and you want that person to get the prime message. Talking about too many issues, in person or in advertising, will confuse the voters and will give the opponent a variety of targets to shoot at, putting your campaign on the defensive. The candidate can deviate the message from location to location by adding a local touch to the speeches. Localized research then becomes an element of candidate advance and campaign volunteer activities.

OPPOSITION RESEARCH

Opposition research is a different animal from issue research and it takes a different kind of volunteer to serve on the opposition research committee. The campaign needs to know all there is to know about probable or actual opponents. Things that should be known are: public, business, professional, educational, political, and personal backgrounds.

Information on potential opponents can be obtained from many sources. Covert activities are not necessary, are usually nonproductive, and they can be counter productive.

Newspapers. Past stories about, and quotes from, opponents can be obtained from the files of newspapers, from libraries, from electronic and other sources. Your political party committee may well keep a current clipping file on your opponent.

Voting Records. If the opponent has served in public office he/

she has a public record. On file will be records of votes, attendance, financial and ethics statements, and more.

Past opponents. People who have run against your opponent in past races are good sources of information about the opponent. Such person may have a box of records in the garage which can be helpful to you. He/she may forewarn you of some tactic that the opponent always uses in his campaigns, or tell you how to get under the opponent's skin. If nothing, else, a person who has run against the opponent before, can tell YOU what kind of campaign to expect.

Personal Contacts. It is amazing how may school chums, fellow workers, etc., will gladly tell you all they know about your opponent. Word of mouth information should not be used without verification.

Political Party Committees. Your political party committees at the national, state and local levels may have opponent research readily available, especially in the general election.

News Conferences and Appearances. Many things said by a candidate in public are never reported in the news media. Having a volunteer or staff member monitor the opponent's news conferences and speaking engagements might just uncover an unexpected quote for use in your campaign. It's also a method of monitoring the opponent for consistency and accuracy.

Campaign Contribution Records. You can tell a lot about an opponent by where his/her money comes from, who the givers are, and how the money is spent. If the opponent has ever sought public office before, campaign contribution and expenditure reports are on file and should be collected and researched.

Summation on Opposition Research. Two important points to remember about opposition research are, 1.) all facts must be checked and double checked. Few things can be more damaging to a campaign than a sensational allegation about an opponent that turns out to be untrue, and 2.) if it's in the public record it's fair game. Using information not in the public record should be a rare exception, not the rule. Accusations about the opponent's personal life are quite often not appreciated by the voting public and can easily backfire.

Opposition research is hard work, but extremely helpful, and it's important to stress quality, not quantity. Whether accomplished by a professional, a staff member or by part-time volunteers, opposition research must be an ongoing campaign project.

CANDIDATE RESEARCH

A similar project to opposition research should be conducted by the campaign on its own candidate. The campaign needs to anticipate and be prepared to answer any charge the opposition might bring to bear on your candidate.

VOTE HISTORY RESEARCH

A knowledge of voting history allows the campaign to target its resources, which are primarily time and money. Targeting allows the campaign the opportunity to concentrate its resources where they can do the most good. The campaign should identify the key voting districts in the primary election, and then a new prioritization needs to take place for the general election. You should break down priority areas to the precinct level, based upon vote history (Republican, Democrat, ticket splitters).

DEMOGRAPHIC RESEARCH

It's wise for the candidate to have a background report on each county describing where the people came from, what they do, average incomes, average educations, etc. Such information can help define and individualize the message and style of campaign appearances. County demographic information is available from the census, libraries, public records, chambers of commerce, past statewide campaigns, etc. Anything noteworthy the candidate has accomplished for the people of each county should also be in the files.

EYEBALL RESEARCH

If observant, the candidate, the campaign driver, the volunteers, the staff and others will see something that can be used as an issue in the campaign. More than likely it will be a local issue, but occasionally it can grow into a broader issue. Examples could be highway maintenance needs, stream pollution, senior citizen housing problems, locales for teenage misconduct, inconsistencies of an opponent's record (says he solved a problem your eyes can see he did not), etc. Eyeball research may seem trite from within an organized campaign structure, but everyone should keep their eyes open.

CONCLUSION

Research is one of those campaign activities that can easily be put aside until later, because the information is often not immediately needed. When such information is needed, however, it's often too late to begin effective research. Not having adequate issue, opponent, or candidate, research information available when it's needed can cost the candidate an opportunity to win the election.

So there you have it. It's not everything you need to know to conduct a successful campaign for public office, but it is a good start. You have a campaign manager, a campaign plan, a finance plan, the beginnings of a campaign organization, you have your message, you know all there is to know about your district and your opponent. To get the job done, you will need a lot of volunteers.

So get busy.

Look at your plan and decide what doors you are going to knock on today. When the door opens, be prepared to explain why you are the best choice, and always ask for the vote.

REMARKS BY MITCHELL E. DANIELS, JR.
L. KEITH BULEN MEMORIAL SERVICE
JANUARY 9, 1999

"O Captain, my Captain! Our fearful trip is done;
  The ship has weather'd every rack, the prize we sought is won....
The ship is anchor'd safe and sound, its voyage closed and done;
  From fearful trip, the victor ship, comes in with object won..."
-Walt Whitman

I learned the single most important lesson of my life in the first half hour I knew Keith Bulen. Like most people here, I continued to learn from Keith for twenty-seven years, right up until last Monday. A few times, I learned what not to say or do. Much more often, the lessons dealt with honor, courage, high goals, keeping your word, and standing by your friends. Those are the lessons he leaves us all, the ones we celebrate today.

A lady friend of Winston Churchill said, "The first time you meet Winston, you see all his faults. Then you spend the rest of your life discovering his virtues." So it seemed with Keith.

Keith could be—let us count the ways—tyrannical and irascible, hotheaded and high-handed, overbearing and domineering, caustic and sarcastic, demanding and demeaning, imperious and impetuous, rude and occasionally even crude . . . and we all loved him.

It's customary at memorial services to reminisce about how the departed friend "touched our lives." I can't really say that about Keith Bulen. Keith didn't touch one's life as much as he invaded, transformed, and sometimes confiscated it. And, somehow, we all loved him for that, too.

What was it that kept political winners, once-weres, and wannabes trooping to his door for a dose of advice or a splash of his blessing, two decades after he retired from politics?

What was it that attracted people of all stations to his projects, got them all moving the same direction, and led so many to surpass themselves in an effort to please him?

Why can no one here fill in this blank? "L. Keith Bulen reminded me a whole lot of _____?"

Maybe one rough comparison would be Vince Lombardi, and it was Lombardi who said "The quality of a person's life is in direct proportion to their commitment to excellence, regardless of their chosen field of endeavor." Surely excellence, always with an overlay of class, was a big part of the Bulen mystique.

Not by accident did the phrase "Bulen operation" become a part of the local vocabulary. (As an aside to the memorial attendees Daniels said, "To those of you standing up today, that's no accident, either. Keith planned this event, and he always taught his advance men to pick a hall that was a little too small for the crowd you expected.") When Keith pulled out the yellow legal pad, you knew it was going to be done right. I'm fond of the saying, "Good enough never is." With Bulen, perfect was almost good enough.

In fact, the only consolation in Keith's preceding us to Heaven's Gate lies in knowing that our own welcoming ceremonies will be impeccably organized. Dick Lugar can probably count on Abraham Lincoln, Teddy Roosevelt, and Dwight Eisenhower in the tarmac receiving line. But they'll have to wait their turn. It will be Keith, of course, first at the foot of the stairs.

Ronald Reagan once said "The real leader is not he who is the greatest doer, but rather he who sets others to doing with the greatest alacrity." It was Keith's magical gift to set others to doing—sometimes by charming them, sometimes by inspiring them, sometimes by terrorizing them.

But after the tirades and the tonguelashings, after the convention or election or the banquet or the weekend was over, everyone involved knew he had been a part of something special, something first-rate and, almost always, something victorious.

With Keith in charge, everybody got a task, a title, a ribbon, a name badge, a committee assignment. Everybody understood that this campaign, and therefore the Republican Party, and therefore the fate of our city, our county, our state, and therefore the future of the United States and all of Western civilization, depended on them, by God. They all went away knowing they were somebody, they were important, they were part of something much bigger than themselves. So they'd damn well better come through. And, over and over, they did. Eagerly. Relentlessly. Overwhelmingly. Joyfully.

Keith didn't do anything halfway, and he didn't let you, either. When he got a hobby, his friends got a new job. Keith receives a UN appointment, and we're all expected to become internationalists. (Before 1970, Gordon Durnil thought ECOSOC was biodegradable footwear.) Keith buys a horse, and overnight we're all standardbred enthusiasts. Keith becomes an International Joint Commissioner, and Canadian water quality vaults past nuclear proliferation as an urgent global priority.

Starting with Keith in 1971 was like joining the Yankees in 1927, or apprenticing Michelangelo in the Sistine Chapel. He was in his absolute prime, and he pushed his troops and himself to the maximum to ensure that Dick Lugar and all he embodied won the greatest victory ever. We still recall it as "the perfect campaign."

My first day of work, Keith sat me down at an old rusty desk with a stack of 29 bios—Dick Lugar's runningmates for the first Unigov Council—and said "OK, kid, you're such a great writer, make 'em all heroes." Actually, he used the term "mummy dummies" in that sentence, but some of them are here today so I did a little editing.

Well, I don't know if my brochures made them heroic, but to me they were, at least collectively. That slate featured a host of talented women, blacks, people in their 20s. A Catholic priest. A community organizer. A professional basketball star. None of today's clever polarization and segmentation for Keith. He wanted every vote in the county; when it was over, his opponents must have felt like he'd nearly gotten them. And he built the kind of Republican party that could compete, year in year out, for the allegiance of literally every citizen, that practiced the politics of addition, not division.

I've tried to recall and explain our love for Keith. Surely part of it was that he loved his friends back so devotedly. Abe Lincoln taught, "Never sell old friends to buy old enemies." Keith's old friends were never for sale; he stood by them, all the more strongly if they were unpopular, down on their luck, or washed up.

And for every tail-chewing or temper tantrum, there were multiple acts of kindness, thoughtfulness, and generosity. He seemed never to overlook a birth or a birthday, a victory or a defeat, a promotion, a grand opening, or an anniversary. His spies—Ruby, Annie, and Sandy—were everywhere, and he made sure they made sure Keith never missed a trick.

I don't think he ever let himself quite believe how much people cared. One night, in a grumpy moment, Keith said to me "One thing for sure, they won't be building any monuments." Now that it's safe to say things like this, "Wrong, boss. Your monuments are everywhere."

One new legacy is the Bulen Symposium on American Politics, created by the good people in this room and dozens of Keith's friends from all over the country.

But what Keith overlooked at the time of his comment was the monuments already in place. Unigov. IUPUI. The new Indianapolis and everything in it. The historic contributions to our nation of Dick Lugar, Bill Ruckelshaus, and countless others whose careers he assisted so instrumentally.

Then there are the leaders yet to come, names we don't even know yet. Because even in the last months of his life, Keith was still scouting for talent, recruiting, counseling, mentoring, and inspiring young people to pursue their ideals in politics and public service. We all got those phone calls that started, "There's a kid I want you to meet. He doesn't know anything, but he's got promise."

So, no, Keith, your judgment failed you this once. These are your monuments, they're all over town, and for my money they're a lot more fitting, and a lot more important, than a name on a street or a statue in a park.

As for me, whatever I'd have done as a career, it wouldn't have included politics, at least in the way it did. Whatever my commitment to truth, honesty, and taking responsibility, it wouldn't have been so deeply engraved on my character. I know there are scores of people here who owe Keith Bulen a similar debt.

Churchill once said, "We are all worms. But I do believe I am a glow worm." Our friend Keith glowed, to say the least; some might say he flamed. It was a flame that warmed us while we had him here, and that will warm us still, in memory, forever.

I'm involved these days in trying to start a new Christian school at 23rd and Park or, as I should say on this occasion, the 3rd Ward, 6th precinct. The other night I learned a lovely phrase from one of my friends at Oasis of Hope Baptist Church, where an event like this one is known as a "homegoing." May we share a word of scripture as we send our friend Keith home:

From Revelations 14 and 21: "And I heard a voice from heaven saying, 'Write this: Blessed are those who die in the Lord . . . that they may rest from their labors . . .'

"And I heard a voice from the throne saying 'He will wipe away every tear from their eyes, and death shall be no more, neither shall there be mourning nor crying nor pain anymore, for the former things have passed away.'"

And from II Timothy 4:6: "For I am now ready to be offered, the hour of my departure is at hand. I have fought the good fight. I have finished my course. I have kept the faith. Hence there is a laid up for me a crown of righteousness which the Lord, a righteous judge, shall give me at that day."

Father, welcome home your good son Keith, who fought his fights well, finished every course, and always kept faith with his friends, his principles, and the code by which he lived. Amen

Mary McCloud, Senator Larry Borst, and Marilyn Smith campaign for Richard Nixon in 1968

Warren Township Republican leadership, 1969

William Ruckelshaus,
Environmental Protection
Agency Director, speaks to
hometown Republicans in
Indianapolis, 1970

Keith Bulen and Gordon Durnil discuss 1970 Indiana Republican State Convention
plans as William D. Ruckelshaus and Dr. Lawrence Borst enjoy a snack.

State Senators John M. Mutz and W. W. Hill, Jr., 1970

The 1970 Open Convention Committee—(seated l-r) Nola Allen, Russell Bontrager, James DuComb, Keith Bulen and Orvas Beers
(standing) Paul Green, Virgil Scheidt, George Glass and Gordon Durnil

Lester Luker and Charles Bogden enjoy chicken at a Republican meeting, 1970

Mayor Lugar, Gordon K. Durnil and Lynda Durnil, 1971

Mayor Lugar, celebrating Indianapolis Award as All American City, 1971

L. Keith Bulen and his team at the 1972 Republican National Convention

Bulen, James Croker, Vice President Agnew, Helen McPherson, George Tintera and Mayor Lugar, 1972

Indianapolis Republican leaders, Larry Wallace, William Spencer and E. Allen Hunter, 1972

John W. Sweezy and Keith Bulen check vote returns on election night, 1972

L. Keith Bulen — 1990

APPENDIX

THE BULEN SYMPOSIUM ON AMERICAN POLITICS COMMENCING DECEMBER 1,1998 INDIANA UNIVERSITY - PURDUE UNIVERSITY AT INDIANAPOLIS

For three decades, L. Keith Bulen personified political leadership in Indiana and far beyond. He served twice in elective office, and served three presidents in major appointive posts, but he will be best remembered for his innovative management of major political campaigns, his leadership in revitalizing the Indiana Republican Party, and his unwavering commitment to the American two-party framework.

His professional passion is matched by his devotion to his alma mater, Indiana University, and to all things traditionally Hoosier. His many admirers from both parties are joining to honor the life and contributions of this great Indiana citizen by creating the Annual Bulen Symposium on American Politics.

One day each year on the campus of IUPUI, political scholars, political practitioners, and journalists will come together to examine the state of the American political system and its two historic parties. A keynote address by a nationally recognized authority will highlight a day of discussion and debate organized around a central topical question.

A committee comprising representatives of the Democratic and Republican parties, the Indiana press corps, and the university community will select topics and speakers. The organizers intend for this program to set a national standard and generate national attention as the foremost convocation of its kind.

YOUR HELP IS NEEDED!

Contributions in support of the Bulen Symposium On American Politics are tax deductible and payable to:

Indiana University Foundation
Bulen Symposium (I32P008173)
P.O. Box 1596
Indianapolis, Indiana 46206-1596
812-855-6310 or toll free at 1-800-558-8311

Profits from this book (if any) will be contributed to the foundation for the symposium fund.

COMMITTEE MEMBERS
THE BULEN SYMPOSIUM ON AMERICAN POLITICS

Chairs:
Mitchell E. Daniels, Jr. and Sheila Suess Kennedy

Co-chairs:

Joseph J. Andrew
Charles Black
Dr. & Mrs. L. M. Borst
John Burkhart
Sandra Donovan
Gordon Durnil
Rex Early
David Frick
Hon. Stephen Goldsmith
Hon. William H. Hudnut, III
Hon. Andy Jacobs, Jr.
Hon. Richard G. Lugar

Michael D. McDaniel
Mr. & Mrs. Owen Meharg
James T. Morris
John Mutz
Dr. Dennis Nicholas
Lyn Nofziger
Hon. Robert D. Orr
Gordon St. Angelo
John Sears
Dr. Beurt SerVaas
John Sweezy

FACULTY FOR FIRST SYMPOSIUM, DECEMBER 1, 1998

IUPUI Chancellor Gerald Bepko, David Broder—*The Washington Post*, Michael D. McDaniel—Indiana GOP Chair, Joe Andrews—Indiana Democratic Chair, Michael Margolis—U of Cincinnati, Martin Wattenberg, U of California-Irvine, Andrew Kohut—Pew Research Center for the People and the Press, Samuel G. Greedman—journalist and author, Mary Beth Schneider—*Indianapolis Star* political columnist, Gordon K. Durnil—former Indiana Republican State Chair and author, and Bill Blomquist—IUPUI. Also, Ted Carmines—Indiana University, Paul Allen Beck—Ohio State University, Brian Vargus—Indiana U Public Opinion Laboratory, Jim Shella—WISH-TV political reporter, James Beatty, Attorney and former Marion County Democratic Chair, Sheila Suess Kennedy—IUPUI assistant professor and author, and Margaret Ferguson—IUPUI.

Republican National Chairman Jim Nicholson, Democratic National Chairman Roy Romer, and commentator Mark Shields. Also, Paul Herrnson—U of Maryland, David Rohde—Michigan State U, Michael Tackett—*The Chicago Tribune*, Mitchell E. Daniels, Jr., Eli Lilly & Co. and former political director for President Reagan, and John Mutz—former Indiana Lt. Governor. David King_Harvard U, Marjorie Hershey—Indiana University, Curtis Gans—Committee for the Study of the American Electorate, Ruy Teixeira—Economic Policy Institute, Ed Paynter—Sierra Club, Jon Schwantes—*Indianapolis Star-News*, and Ken Bode—Northwestern U and Washington Week in Review on PBS.

MORE ABOUT KEITH

L. KEITH BULEN
BACKGROUND INFORMATION

Born: December 31, 1926 - Madison County, Indiana
Deceased January January 4, 1999, Johnson County, Indiana

Family:

Children:
Leslie K. (b. 1951)
Bachelor's Degree—Indiana University
Masters Degree—Indiana University
Married to Dr. Mark Mills

Lisa K. (b. 1965)
Bachelor's Degree—Nursing, University of Miami, Coral Gables, Florida
Married to Steve Rodda

L. Kassee (b. 1973)
Bachelor's Degree—Ball State University

L. Kellee (b. 1975)
Graduate—Indiana University School of Nursing
    Pediatric Surgical Nurse, Riley Hospital for Children

Granddaughters:

Lawren K. Mills (b. 1978) Attending DePauw University

Lindsey K. Rodda (b. November 28, 1998)

Education: Pendleton High School, 1944
Indiana University, 1949—Bachelor's Degree (Government)
Indiana University School of Law, 1952—Doctor of Jurisprudence—Top 1/3

Military: Enlisted Army Air Force, World War II
Service: Overseas—5th Air Force-Commissioned 1949.

Occupation: Former Senior Member, Law firm of: Bulen, Castor, Robinette and Nickels

Member: American, 7th Circuit, Indiana, Indianapolis and U.S. Supreme Court Bar, Past President, Indianapolis Lawyers Association.

ACTIVELY ENGAGED IN POLITICS AND GOVERNMENT FOR FORTY-FIVE YEARS

Elected and/or appointed to serve at Block, Precinct, Ward, District, County, State, National and International levels. Elected Delegate to the Republican State Convention, 1954 through 1980. Chairman of Credentials Committee, 1966, 1968 and 1970. Honored Platform Guest 1962-78; Honorary Chairman, 1984

Unanimously elected Chairman of Marion County Republican Central Committee, 1966, 1968 and 1970, Indianapolis, Indiana, winning every City and County election 1966-72.

Elected 11th Congressional District Chairman, 1966, 1972 and 1974, Indianapolis, Indiana.

Member of G.O.P. Indiana State Central Committee, State Executive Committee, State Rules Committee, State Budget Committee, State Campaign Committee, Executive Committee of State Campaign Committee, Republican State Citizens Finance Executive Committee, 1966 to 1974.
Elected Republican National Committeeman for Indiana, 1968; re-elected unanimously, 1972.
Elected to Executive Committee of Republican National Committee, 1969; re-elected 1972.
State Nixon for President Coordinator, 1968 and 1972.
Elected Delegate to Republican National Convention, 1968, 1972, 1976, 1980 and 1984. Indiana Delegation Co-Chairman and Caucus Chairman, 1972.
Member, Arrangements Committee, 1972 Republican National Convention.
Chairman of Nixon-Bowen Victory Committee, 1972.
Chairman, Indiana Presidential Inaugural Committee, 1969 and 1973.
Campaign Chairman, Mayor Richard G. Lugar, Indianapolis, 1967 and 1971.
    Campaign Chairman, Senator Richard G. Lugar, U.S. Senate Campaign, 1974.
Member, Steering Committee, Midwest Republican Conference, 1970-1974.
Chairman, Republican Midwest Conference, 14 States, 1971.
District Congressional Young Republican Chairman and State Young Republican Central Committee.
Past President, Marion County Republican Veterans.
Deputy Marion County Coroner, 1960—1992.
Elected to Indiana House of Representatives, 1960.
Re-elected to House of Representatives, 1962; served as Chairman of Marion County Delegation, Member of State Republican Legislative Policy Committee, and Chairman of other permanent Legislative Committees. Chairman of

State Courts and Criminal Law Commission, 1960 through 1964.

U.S. Delegate to Economic and Social Council of the United Nations, 49th Session; Geneva, Switzerland, 1970. Reappointed Delegate to 55th Session; Geneva, Switzerland, 1973. U.S. Observer to United Nations Natural Resources Conference, Nairobi, Kenya, Africa, 1972. Attended U.N. Security Council Meeting, Addis Ababa, Ethiopia, Africa, January, 1972.

Former Marion County Deputy Prosecutor, 1952-60.

Indianapolis Chamber of Commerce Chairman, Law Enforcement Division, 1960-64

Member of Greater Indianapolis Progress Committee, Inc.

Member, Governor's Task Force for Employment of the Handicapped for Indiana.

Member, Advisory Board on Urban Affairs, University of Indianapolis

Antelope Club Man of the Year.

Member, U.S. Department of Justice Unit of the National Defense Executive Reserve.

Indiana Study Commission for Campaign and Financing Reform, 1974.

Coordinator of successful Reagan Indiana Presidential Campaign Primary, 1976 and 1980; Honorary Co-Chairman, 1984.

National G.O.P. Convention Coordinator of six Midwest states for Governor Reagan-1976.

Deputy Chairman, National Reagan for President Committee, 1979-80.

1980 Reagan for President National Convention Director

1980 Reagan-Bush Eastern Coordinator (17 states).

Associate Director of Presidential Personnel, Office of the President-Elect.

Citizens for the Republic Steering Committee.

Twice, Indianapolis Junior Chamber of Commerce Good Government Award nominee.

First Recipient of Richard Smith Memorial Award by Young Republican National Federation–1978.

Indianapolis Junior Chamber of Commerce Good Government Recipient–1972.

Honorary Doctorate of Humanities, Vincennes University.

Indiana Republican Mayors Association Man of the Year - 1972.

Sigma Nu Alumni of the Year, Indiana University Chapter, Alumni Hall of Fame–1983.

Kentucky Colonel by Governor Louie B. Nunn.

Commissioned Admiral in the Texas Navy.

Sagamore of the Wabash by Governor Edgar D. Whitcomb.

Sagamore of the Wabash by Governor Otis R. Bowen.

Sagamore of the Wabash by Governor Robert D. Orr.

Sagamore of the Wabash by Governor Frank O'Bannon

The Order of the Paul Revere Patriots by Governor John A. Volpe of Massachusetts.

Murat Shrine—Past President, Murat Chanters: Past President, Great Lakes Shrine Chanters Association; Past President, Caravan Club; Member, Kowalk Al'Sabikin; Former Potentate's Aide.

Wendell Wilkie Centennial Celebration, National Advisory Committee.

Sigma Nu Fraternity Board of Directors.

Phi Delta Phi Legal Fraternity.

Southport Christian Church.

Columbia Club.

Englewood Lodge.

Hoosier Hundred and I.U. lifetime Alumni.

Director, Marion County Republican Veterans.

Capitol Hill Club.

Homeowners Association.

The American Legion.

Member—American Association of Political Consultants.

Appointed by President Reagan to the International Joint Commission, United States and Canada, and confirmed by the U.S. Senate–1981. Principal in Bulen–Olson Treaty between US and Canada (Washington State and Province of British Columbia), 1984.

October, 1984; Chairman of "Integrated Transboundary Monitoring Network–A Continuing Binational Exploration" Workshop, National Academy of Natural Sciences of Philadelphia, Pennsylvania.

Senior Commissioner, International Joint Commission

June 1985, Chairman of Great Lakes Levels Seminar, Kingston, Ontario.

Mr. Bulen is listed in Who's Who in the U.S., in the Midwest, and in Politics.

1987-88: Cabinet Member John Mutz for Governor

1987-88; Senior Advisor, National Bush for President Campaign

1989-90 Chairman, Victory '90 Indiana House and Senate Campaign Committee

1990–92 Elected Indiana House of Representatives Served as ranking member Urban Affairs, Environmental Affairs and Governmental Affairs Committees. Also Legislative Advisory Commission for the Indiana State Fair Board.

1992–Elected only life time member of Greater Indianapolis Republican Finance Committee Chairman's Club

1994–Senior Consultant to Newman for Marion County Prosecutor Committee.

1996–Installed "Hall of Fame " Royal Order of Loyal Republicans by MCRCC and GIRFCO.

ACTIVELY ENGAGED IN STANDARDBRED HORSE RACING AND BREEDING

Bulen has raced and/or bred such outstanding pacers as Abercrombie, And Fitch, Dancer, Donovan, Incomparable, Indiana Ab, Ultra Osborne, Armbro Debra, Shadow's Graham, Lady Nancy R., Ab's Comet, Happy Hoosier, Marvin Wood, Foxy First Lady, Blitzen, George W, Sir Abercrombie, Mid Western Charm, Lulabula and many others. Member of the U.S., Indiana, Ohio, Ontario, Illinois, Michigan, Canadian, Maryland, Kentucky, Delaware, New Jersey, New York, Pennsylvania, etc., Trotting and Pacing Associations. Mr. Bulen owned world champion, Abercrombie, voted Harness Horse of the Year in 1978 and world leading money winning sire.

1986–90, Indiana Horse Hall of Fame-1992.
1992-93 Incorporator and elected to Board of Directors Standardbred Owners and Breeders of Indiana Inc.
1995–Elected Director (4 year term) Indiana Standardbred Association.
1996-Elected President of Indiana Standardbred Association.
1997-Inducted "Indiana Standardbred Hall of Fame"
1997-Indiana Standardbred Association's "Lifetime Achievement Award"

Index

A

Abercrombie 3, 89, 208, 209
Agnew, Spiro T. 47, 199
Allebrandi, Tom 119
Allen, Nola 16, 42, 55, 67, 196
Andrew, Joe 160, 204
Apple, Johnny 116
Applegate, Charles W. 11, 12, 66, 69
Armantrout, Alice 13
Armstrong, Fred L. 66, 69, 119

B

Barbour, Walter H. 12
Barton, John J. 10, 144
Bayh, Birch 44, 73, 85, 86, 146
Beatty, James 144, 204
Beck, Paul Allen 159, 204
Beckman, Robert 31
Beckman, Robert D., Jr 68
Beckweth, Robbie 76
Beers, Orvas E. 36, 41, 43, 39, 51, 55, 196
Bell, Avis C. 76
Bell, Mark 76
Bennent, Scotty 70, 76
Bepko, Gerald 204
Black, Charles 122, 203
Bliss, Ray 16, 74, 77
Block Captain 31
Blomquist, Bill 204
Bode, Ken 204
Bontrager, Russell 196
Borst, Lawrence M. 11, 12, 66, 111, 194, 195, 203
Bosma, Charles E. 12
Boundary Waters Treaty of 1909 133
Bowen, Otis R. "Doc" 76, 81, 82, 86, 97, 102, 104, 129, 206, 207,
Bradford, Cale vii, 138

Branigin, Roger D. 39
Bray, William G. 83
Brinkman, Joyce 107
Broder, David 159, 204
Brown, H. Dale 10, 13, 76
Brown, Roger W. 76
Bruce, Donald 113
Buck, James A. 11
Buell, Lawrence L. 69
Bulen, L. Kassee 205
Bulen, L. Kellee 205
Bulen-Olson Treaty 136
Burkhart, John
    vii, 11, 19, 68, 114, 141, 203
Burton, Dan 14, 12, 13,
    107, 111, 151, 152
Bush, George vii, 1, 4, 90, 121
busing school children 75
Butler University 36
Butz, Earl L. 97, 100

C

Caito, Thomas A. 76
Camp, Lucille 66, 69
Campaign Communicators, Inc. 80
Capehart, Homer 85
Carmines, Ted 204
Castor, Charles G. 69, 205
Chambers, Bob 120
Chumley, Dell 70
Churchill, Winston 45, 189
Citizens for Nixon-Agnew 45
Claffey, Carol 13
Clark, Alex M. 9, 10, 19, 20, 21, 22, 24, 144, 155
Clayburgh, Dr. Ben 119
Clinton, President 89
Colbert, Bill 31, 120, 121
Coleman, Muriel D. 118, 122
College For Political Knowledge 51
Colwell, Jack vii, 91, 93
Conn, Harriett B. 12
Cox, Don 103, 104
Croker, James 199
Crow, Ray P. 12